'DESPISE IT NOT'

A Hull man spies on the Kaiser's Germany

Ian Sumner

Highgate of Beverley

Highgate Publications (Beverley) Limited
2002

ACKNOWLEDGEMENTS

I would like to thank all who have helped with the writing of this book, but particularly my wife Maggie, the families of the descendants of Max Schultz, especially Molly Megson and Barbara Grimm, Alan Judd, John Markham, and the staffs of Beverley and Hull Local Studies Libraries, Leeds University Library and the Public Record Office.

British Library Cataloguing in Publication Data.
A catalogue record for this book is available from the British Library.

ISBN 1 902645 34 0

Published by

Highgate of Beverley

Highgate Publications (Beverley) Limited
4 Newbegin, Beverley, HU17 8EG. Telephone (01482) 886017

Printed by Highgate Print Limited
4 Newbegin, Beverley, HU17 8EG. Telephone (01482) 886017

PROLOGUE: A MODEL

In May 1999, a Hamburg postal worker, Detlev Knölke, was spending some time at an antiques market in Schenefeld, in the western suburbs of his home city. On one stall he saw an old model of a ship, a liner by her looks, her three slightly raked funnels, tall superstructure and a straight stem all suggesting a pre-First World War vessel. The model itself was crudely made, perhaps not a craftsman's job, and time had not been kind to it. Yet it had been made with some attention to detail, as if someone had tried to get everything right, but had been defeated by his tools or materials. Looking more closely, painted on the hull was the name *Imperator* – a liner, indeed, the pride of the Hamburg-Amerika Line, launched in 1913 by the Kaiser himself, and one of the biggest ships in the world in her day. Herr Knölke decided to buy it, at a cost of 180 Marks (about £60).

The proud owner had a friend who was something of a ship modeller,

Max's model of the German liner Imperator, *seen before its restoration.*

and, what was more, had also served aboard the ships of the Hamburg-Amerika Line. Peter Blühm, the former merchant marine officer, set about the tricky task of restoring the model to its former glory. The ship's boats had been made from thin sheet lead, and were all bent out of shape. The funnels . . . ah, the foremost funnel was loose, no, removable. Underneath lay a small piece of wood covered with fine grit glued down to represent coal, and that too was removable. Underneath that was . . . a folded piece of brittle brown paper. Curious, Blühm opened it to find a note in pencil. It was written in English by the man who had made the model. Blühm could not read the language, but, anxious to know more about the writer, he approached the local newspaper, which translated it for him. The author of the note was Max William Schultz, an Englishman, serving time in the prison at Fuhlsbüttel, near Hamburg.

And Max William Schultz was a spy.

1

AN IMMIGRANT FAMILY

Max Wilhelm Emil Hugo Schultz (to give him his full name) was born in Hull on 3 March 1875, the second child of Rudolf Schultz and his wife Luise. Rudolf had been born in 1841, in the town of Landsberg, lying on the River Warthe, part of the German state of Prussia (now known as Gorzów Wielkopolski, in western Poland). Rudolf's wife Luise (née Zimmermann) was born further west, in the Baltic seaport of Rostock, in 1844. Rudolf was a shoemaker, and had to travel to wherever he could find work. The couple's first child, Carl, had been born in another Baltic seaport, Wismar, in 1871, but, before they emigrated to Hull, they had a boot and shoe shop in the port of Swinemünde (also now in Poland, and known as Swinoujscie), situated on the island of Usedom at the mouth of the River Oder. We do not know exactly why Rudolf and Luise decided to emigrate. It may well have been motivated by simple poverty, or perhaps a search for wider horizons – Pomerania, that part of Prussia which was his home, was noted for its thin, sandy soils, scoured by winds from the Arctic, and its solid, dependable young men, driven off the land by poor returns, had provided the backbone of the Prussian Army since the days of Frederick the Great, over a hundred years before. Certainly Pomerania had not benefited from industrialisation to the same extent of other areas further south, such as the Ruhr. But even these prosperous districts were surprised by a sudden recession in both manufacturing industry and agriculture which struck Germany in 1873, and which was to last for the rest of the decade.

Germans had been living in Hull since the Middle Ages. From as early as the thirteenth century, much of Hull's trade lay with the countries which bordered the North Sea and the Baltic, and it is scarcely surprising that there would be some, Germans, Dutch or Dane, who came to England to represent their own interests in a foreign port. However, the mid-nineteenth century saw a significant increase in the number of Germans coming to live in this country. Some came for economic reasons, prompted by the relaxation of duties relating to the import of goods in 1848, for Britain's advanced economy offered opportunities, even for the small businessman and craftsman, which were not available on the more conservative mainland of Europe. Others emigrated for political reasons – the crushing of a number of liberal revolutions in 1848 had led to a flood of refugees into Great Britain, all seeking a haven from repression at home.

Hull became one of the main ports of entry for immigrants from Germany and the rest of Northern Europe, partly because of the well-established links and frequent sailings between Hull and Hamburg. By German law, German immigrants could only be carried in German-owned ships; whilst the Hull-based Wilson Line had a monopoly of the Scandinavian immigrant trade. (It is ironic to note that, when the Wilson Line was sold in 1916, it was bought by John Reeves Ellerman, whose father, Johan Herman Ellermann, had arrived in Hull from Hamburg in 1850.) Conditions on these immigrant ships, even on the relatively short North Sea crossing, left a great deal to be desired, with overcrowding all too frequent. The 578-ton barque, *Alster*, owned by the Hamburg company E. Hagen, arrived in Hull in April 1881, just as the Census was being taken, and managed to cram 130 passengers into her 143-feet length – in addition to storage and the crew's quarters. For many ship owners and captains, immigrants were just a cargo like any other, in some cases mere ballast for returning grain ships.

Some of these immigrants were cheated. There were those who had bought tickets for America, only to be told that they were valid only as far as Hull; on arrival in Hull, others were told that they had indeed landed in America! Some carried on, making their own way to Liverpool; others stayed, perhaps in Hull, or in the towns of the West Riding, particularly in Bradford. For those who decided to remain in Hull, conditions were atrocious. Most of the immigrants (around 85% of the foreign-born families who were listed in the 1881 Census) found accommodation within an area extending only half a mile of the docks. Hull had its 'Little Ireland', but, unlike Bradford, no 'Little Germany'. Congregated pell-mell in Hull's rookeries were people from all four corners of England, Scotland, Ireland and Wales, and from further afield, from Havana in Cuba to Hardanger in Norway, from Marseilles in France to Mariopol in Russia – among them the Italian organ grinder, the American 'nigger comedian', and, of course, the German shoemaker.

Prompted by an outbreak of scarlet fever in 1881, which killed 689 children, mostly under the age of five, and a mortality rate from infantile diarrhoea which averaged 311 deaths a year, one correspondent of the Hull newspaper the *Eastern Morning News* took it upon himself to survey housing conditions in the worst affected areas. Writing of the St. James district, which bordered the area where Rudolf and Luise had settled, he declared that 'all the perfumes of Araby would not sweeten this district, all the waters of the Jordan would not consecrate it to Christian service'. A small square on The Ropery, he claimed 'for accumulated filth and squalor, rotting timbers and crumbling brickwork, unpicturesque wretchedness and abandonment, will certainly bear comparison with the foulest slums of Constantinople'.

But he was not finished. Warming to his theme, he turned his wrath on an area that he called the Rabbit Warrens. 'Never did a place better deserve the name,' he thundered. 'Rounded by [Great] Passage Street and Osborne Street, and by Upper Union Street and Fawcett Street, it consists of narrow covered entries, long unvisited by pavior or whitewasher, leading to cross courts, intersected by filthy privies so planted that privacy is all-but impossible, and constructed so as to exclude as much light and air from the wretched dwellings as possible. The drains and watertaps are expected to respond to unlimited demands, with the usual result. Some of the blind alleys are in a

The three Schultz children, taken in about 1885 – from left to right: Carl, Clara and Max, who was then ten years old.

horribly disgusting state; no doubt partly because the people are far from particular in their habits – how, indeed, can the inhabitants of this den be expected to cherish sentiments of decency and self-respect? The district is specially cared for in the matters of public houses, of course. They rejoice in the possession and adornment of the main thoroughfare corners; they are the choice buildings in the adjoining streets, and they stand like sentinels at the entering in of the courts. They accumulate while men decay; their owners fatten on the vice and thriftlessness engendered by such surroundings . . . We turn into Osborne Street, noting on the way that every corner, as a rule, is a place licensed for the sale of drink, besides the interim resting places which flaunt their warmth and brightness to the dismal courts. "Back way to the Beehive" or to a similar place is often the inscription which meets the eye and the red lamp at the end of the court emphasises the tacit invitation. The prime consideration in the building of these courts has been the crowding of as many habitations as possible into a limited space. The whole district requires overhauling – it reeks with a foulness, and the marvel is that fever is not a constant guest, the welcome being so warm.'

Here then were Rudolf and his family. In 1881, they were living at 4 Marine Row, Great Passage Street, a tight row of houses between two of Hull's main arteries, Anlaby Road and Hessle Road, and just across the street from those very Rabbit Warrens. Did their hearts sink when they saw the area where they were to make their home? Did they think, however briefly, that no matter how bad things had been in Pomerania, they had never reached this level? Son Carl had now been joined by Max and their sisters Louisa (born 1876) and Clara (born 1878). Rudolf was a shoemaker, but it would appear that he was unable to bring in enough money on his own account to support his family, so there were no fewer than nine lodgers in the house, all seamen – six Germans, two Norwegians and an American.

Having this source of extra income was essential to the family, since the mid-1880s was a time of deep economic recession in Hull, which brought many to the verge of starvation. East Park was first laid out at this time, partly to provide jobs for the unemployed; but even this was not always enough, with many of the labourers collapsing, weak through malnutrition, to be replaced by single men, often from the country areas of the East Riding, used to hard work in the open air. The Park was thus laid out and the project completed, but it had failed in its attempt at poor relief within the town. The winters were particularly bad, since the number of ships inbound from such places as the Baltic fell off considerably, and many casual labourers in the docks and shipyards were laid off as a consequence. Yet despite the harsh economic climate, despite the poverty and the poor housing

Max when a young man.

conditions, more immigrants, by now largely Polish and Baltic Jews displaced by pogroms, continued to arrive in the town.

Max, then, was brought up in a German family, in a German community in a British town. Like Max's father, the other members of Hull's German community were mostly small tradesmen, particularly tailors, but also butchers, bakers and other craftsmen. Given that most emigrants left their country by sea, it is perhaps not surprising that many of the German population of Hull continued to come from the north of the country, particularly from those areas which, like Pomerania, bordered on the Baltic Sea coast (although the city was also home to a small community of Württembergers, from the south-west of Germany). Those whose fortunes had improved and who had acquired sufficient wealth to afford servants often employed people from the same town as themselves, possibly from a family connection, or perhaps simply from sentiment. They were able to move out from the immediate centre of the city, further westwards down Anlaby Road, or towards Spring Bank. Rudolf and Luise, however, appear to have had no prior connection with Hull – certainly, Rudolf was the only person from Landsberg in the city.

By the 1890s, Germans formed the largest immigrant group in the town, with nearly 1,000 people, a figure equivalent to one-third of all Hull's immigrants. There was a German Working Man's Club from as early as the 1860s. Its secretary, one Gustav Schmidt, was also active in the Furniture Workers' Union, in an industry that employed a number of his countrymen as cabinetmakers. Given that some of the immigrants were political refugees, it is not surprising that there was also a small political society, the Club Freiheit ('Freedom Club'), which included amongst its membership a number of anarchists and socialists, whose clashes, both verbal and physical, made the pages of the local press. To cater for the spiritual life of the immigrant community, German Lutheran services were held initially at the Mariners' Church on Posterngate; from 1848 services were held at the Sailors' Institute, and finally at the Bethesda Chapel in Osborne Street (not far from the Schultzs' house). The church found a permanent home in 1859 when the congregation bought the disused St. Luke's Church in nearby Nile Street. The new church attracted between one and two hundred regular communicants and ran a well-attended Sunday School. That the congregation could do this by raising a loan suggests that the German community in Hull was becoming increasingly wealthy and self-confident.

By 1891, the Schultz family were living at 7 Osborne Street, not very far away from their last address. Things were perhaps now a little easier for the family, since both sons were now working: Carl, who had anglicised his name to Charles, was a cabinetmaker, whilst Max was an apprentice at Earle's Shipyard. Even so, they were still taking in lodgers – eight this time, all German seamen.

The family were soon on the move again, not long after the 1891 Census was taken, this time to 28 Adelaide Street (still in the same area, but perhaps a little 'better' socially). It would appear that they had decided to stay in the country where they had first arrived, for Rudolf, Luise and Carl / Charles had all become naturalised British citizens. Despite the unpromising nature of their original surroundings, the family would seem to have found a home in the town. By the end of Victoria's reign, figures drawn from the 1901 Census suggest that the German community in Hull was in decline, with less than 20% of immigrants listed as German-born, but this figure conceals the true picture, for many immigrants had children who had been born in this country (like Max and his two sisters) who counted as British.

It is difficult to generalise about the feelings of immigrants towards their adopted country, and how their sentiments may have differed from those of their children who were born in this country. So much must have depended on individual circumstances, and on the attitudes of both parents and children. Max's own feelings are discussed later

The Schultz family in 1893: Rudolf, Luise and Max at the back, Clara and Carl at the front.

in the book. Two members of the Hohenrein family, whose grandparents had originally come to Hull from Württemberg in the 1840s or early 1850s, certainly thought themselves so thoroughly British that they joined the Territorial Army – one in the East Riding Yeomanry, and the other in the Army Service Corps – and, from their appearance in photographs, were proud to have done so. On the outbreak of war in 1914, a considerable number of naturalised citizens presented a memorial to the city's Lord Mayor, protesting their loyalty to Britain.

Whether their opinion of themselves was reciprocated by their neighbours is open to question. When a man named Rudolph Lehmann was selected as Liberal candidate to contest the 1886 Election for Central Hull, one newspaper, the *Hull and East Riding Critic*, scoffed that it was 'afraid that Mr. Lehmann's nationality will not be a recommendation for him in the eyes of the electors. They don't appreciate anything German – from sausages to itinerant brass bands.' This gratuitous insult reveals that anti-German hostility did indeed exist at this time in Hull (ill-informed hostility at that, since Lehmann had been born in Sheffield). German immigrants were electorally insignificant as a group; the number of immigrants who had become naturalised citizens was quite small – only about 10% of the total – and only men had the vote, which reduced their numbers still further, to a point where the *Critic* clearly felt that it could abuse them freely without any kind of electoral repercussions.

But, at a day-to-day level, practical businessmen could not allow themselves to be swayed by such prejudice. By 1913, Germany imported 763,206 tons of coal shipped through Hull; indeed, it was the second most important destination for outgoing goods. Further, trade with Germany accounted for 11% of the total inward and outward tonnage, second only to Russia, and Russia-bound ships had to pass through the Kiel Canal to ensure a swift passage to and from their destination. The Hull Chamber of Commerce and Shipping even printed a German introduction to their guide to the port in the hope of attracting further business.

2

A BUSINESSMAN

Max married Sarah Hilton at St. Luke's Church, Hull, on 26 January 1894. Sarah was the daughter of George and Elizabeth Hilton. George Hilton was a prosperous fish merchant, originally from Great Yarmouth, who lived in Goodwin Street, with premises in the covered market in the centre of the town. He was sufficiently well-off to own a large house in Scarborough, as well as retaining property in his native town, and a chain of smokehouses along the east coast. In Hull, he later formed a partnership with the Moody brothers, as fish, game and poultry dealers, in the covered market on Park Street. Sarah thus came from a prosperous background, and Max must have seemed like

Sarah and the children: from left to right, Clara, George, Gladys, Sarah, Lily (standing) and Beatrice.

a man with good prospects. Max and Sarah were to have eight children altogether, of whom five survived infancy: Lily Mary (born in 1895), Beatrice, nicknamed 'Beatrice Lee' by her father, but known to the rest of the family as Beattie (born 1899), Gladys Victoria (1901), Clara (1905) and George (born in 1908). Their first house was 43 Goodwin Street in Hull, near Max's father-in-law.

Max moved from building ships at Earle's to selling them, describing himself as a yacht broker. As a yacht broker, his job was to buy and sell yachts, and by far the most important part of the country for yachting was the Solent. Racing took place on the estuary from May until autumn, but the most important races were held during Cowes Regatta Week in August. The Regatta was organised by the Royal Yacht Squadron, whose patron since 1863 had been the Prince of Wales (later Edward VII). The small castle-like club house at West Cowes on the Isle of Wight became the centre of the social world, as great yachts came from all over the globe, to race, or just to see and be seen. The local newspaper, the *Isle of Wight Herald*, devoted almost as much space to fashion as it did to the racing: 'Lady Pentland in black with a knot of pink flowers . . . the Misses Bulkeley dressed alike in dark blue serge and rough straw hats, trimmed in front with grey gulls' wings . . . Mrs. Horace Ricardo quietly attired in black . . . the Countess of Normanton and Mrs. Patrick de Bathe were charmingly costumed in pale grey . . .' and so on.

Edward, both as Prince and later as King, gave Cowes Week its elevated social status, and so, by extension, the whole sport of yacht racing. The week's events attracted members of high society from all over Europe: on occasion the Tsar of Russia would visit, the German Emperor was a regular attendee, as was the King of Spain, and yachtsmen from the United States, Norway, Sweden, Denmark, France and Holland. But at this level yachting was undoubtedly a rich man's hobby. The Prince of Wales's yacht *Britannia* (not the vessel recently retired and now at Leith) cost its owner £8,000 when it was built in 1893, the equivalent of over £300,000 at current prices.

Other centres, such as the River Clyde in Scotland, Kiel in Germany, and the fashionable seaside resort of Ostend in Belgium, tried to copy Cowes, but none quite managed to match its social success and standing. Kiel Week (in June), it is true, attracted many American millionaires such as J. P. Morgan, Cornelius Vanderbilt and Andrew Carnegie, who used yachting as another way to demonstrate their phenomenal riches, and who were flattered to be invited by the Kaiser Wilhelm himself.

The Kaiser was one of the principal supporters of yachting in Germany. A troubled man in so many ways, he sought an area of life in which he could triumph over his 'Uncle Bertie', King Edward VII.

But there were other reasons for his enthusiasm for the sport. The noted yachtsman Anthony Heckstall-Smith recalled a conversation that took place between his father, a famous yachtsman in his day, and Prince Heinrich of Prussia, the brother of the Kaiser. The Prince began, 'The Germans are not a yachting nation. They were not really, until lately, a seafaring nation. It is only my brother's interest in yachting that causes our people to go in for the sport. They go in for it because they are obliged to, to please him. He wishes them to take to yachting and make "Kiel Week" a sort of "Cowes Week" in order to encourage them to take an interest in the navy. You see, we have to get money for the navy, and the nation knows nothing about navies or the sea. Half of them have never seen the sea. But if they go to the seaside and read about the Emperor's yacht and so forth, and the wealthy merchants who know nothing of the sport try to become yachtsmen to please the Emperor, then it stirs up interest in seafaring pursuits and we can get money for the navy. There's no doubt about it, our people buy yachts and race them to please my brother. I dare say they get very sea-sick!'

The Germans may not have been enthusiastic yachtsmen, but many were enthusiastic courtiers. The owner of the Hamburg-Amerika Line, Albert Ballin, had one of his old liners, the *Deutschland*, converted into a yacht-cum-floating hotel for the Kiel Week of 1912. Renamed the *Viktoria Luise*, after the Kaiser's only daughter, the ship accommodated an immense party of the Kaiser's guests, all at the expense of Ballin, who was left with a bill equivalent to nearly a quarter of a million pounds at to-day's prices. Ballin was a very wealthy man of course: after the launch of the *Imperator* in 1913, he immediately had laid down another, bigger, liner – the immense, even more luxurious *Vaterland*.

Yachting circles, then, included a lot of people with a lot of money to spend. And into these waters sailed Max. He had knowledge of shipbuilding gained through his apprenticeship, and he had a ready charm. He was a short stocky man, only 167cm and weighing 86kg (or, in pre-metrication terms, five feet six inches tall, and thirteen stones seven pounds in weight), with light brown hair and grey eyes. He was always immaculately dressed, and always, as his daughter Gladys recalled, smelled of pomade and cigars.

He first went into partnership with a Goole shipbroker, Walter H. Smith, who lived at Belsize House, on Hook Road, on the outskirts of the town. But Smith died in 1909, and Max was left to continue on his own account. Some of the boats he sold appear in the pages of *Lloyd's Register of Yachts*. These must represent only some of the vessels he bought and sold – possibly those he could not sell on immediately. All appear to be older boats – the motor schooner *Lizzie* was built on the

Clyde in 1878, whilst a similar vessel, the *Lotus*, was built in Liverpool in the same year; another craft, *Forest Fly*, was built in Dartmouth in 1881. His customers included the Marquess of Exeter, who bought the *Lotus*, and a William O'Meara of Southampton, who purchased both the *Lizzie* and *Forest Fly* from Max in the same year. From the evidence of these craft, then, Max does not appear to have been catering to yacht racers but those who simply liked to cruise in their boats, or perhaps those who bought them as a fitting ornament to their leisured lifestyle. Max acquired a yacht of his own, the *Lady Esmerelda* (this was also his pet name for his daughter Gladys), but strangely never seems to have registered it. He even took part in the racing, and once won a trophy consisting of a silver anchor on a blue velvet background, all within a frame – a trophy that once had pride of place in the family home.

Throughout this time, Max appears to have conducted his business from his house in Goodwin Street. But as much of his business was with the Solent sailing set, in 1910 he opened a small office in Southampton, at 2 St. Michael's Street, presumably to be closer to his clients. He appears to have been successful in his business, for he employed a number of people. Amongst them was John Constant, his manager (summed up by Max as 'a good friend and an excellent businessman'), and someone, perhaps a clerk, but given the standard of his spelling in a letter to the German prison authorities, more likely a crewman, by the name of James Englefield. Yet much of Max's early life remains a mystery. He certainly travelled a lot and was no stranger to trouble. His German prison record reveals that his head bore the scars of a beating with a cane, his right hand bore a scar from a knife wound received in a brawl on board a ship off the coast of Africa in 1903; he also carried a wound in his right thigh. In 1908-9 he was certainly in the Mediterranean, for he was in the port of Messina in the aftermath of its terrible earthquake of December 1908.

Yet, for all that, Max was a fond, if frequently absent, father. He was in Greece when his son George was born. Even though he was so many miles away, he directed a stream of telegrams to Coltman Street, one of which read, 'I am drinking the boy's health in champagne.' Sadly, the birth was so difficult that Sarah was in no fit condition to read them, and to the midwives they were just an annoying distraction. Max's absences meant that George Hilton became a substitute father to his grandchildren.

Max was certainly successful enough in his business to enable his family to move home, to 82 Coltman Street in 1907. Coltman Street was thought of at the time as a 'good address'. 'I remember every inch of the house,' recalled Max's eldest granddaughter, Mary Stevenson. 'It had a separate entrance, with an elegant hall and staircase.' All the rooms were large, with high ceilings. The drawing room accommodated a floor-to-ceiling painting in the classical style, as well as a large ebony upright piano, whilst the dining room displayed a huge painting of the market place at Messina. Each of the children had their own room, and there were no fewer than three maids: Kate Aycock, her younger sister Alice, and Polly Button.

By this time, however, the Schultz family had broken up and gone their separate ways. Max's parents and sister had moved back to Germany – indeed, back to Swinemünde. His mother died there in 1903. Clara married a local man, a senior pilot by the name of Modrow.

The Schultz's house in Coltman Street.

13

3
ENTER 'C'

Rivalry between Britain and Germany developed in the third quarter of the nineteenth century, and intensified as the century drew to a close. Industry was developing more quickly in Germany than in Britain, and its companies sought new outlets for their products, particularly outside Europe. Consequently, Germany had established her first colonies in Africa and the South Pacific in the 1880s. To defend these new ventures, some politicians thought it necessary to build a strong navy, a policy supported by the Kaiser himself. Germany saw Britain as its main rival in trade and industry. British policy, however, was designed to ensure that the growing German navy could never challenge its own long-established supremacy. A strategy of maintaining the Royal Navy at something more than the combined strength of the navies of its two most powerful rivals – the so-called 'two power standard' – had served Britain well down the years. All this was to change, however, with the launch of the battleship H.M.S. *Dreadnought* in 1906.

The launch of the *Dreadnought* marked a momentous change in the development of warships. The power and arrangements of the ship's main guns, and its reliance on oil-fired turbines rather than coal-fired boilers, gave the new vessel a much superior fighting power, as well as improved speed and endurance. But the ship was so advanced and so powerful for its day that it instantly rendered obsolete all other battleships, even British ones. This meant that the numerical superiority of the Royal Navy, so patiently built up over the preceding century, was immediately nullified, and smaller powers suddenly found themselves at the same level as the Royal Navy, which was in effect starting from scratch. As the British built new *Dreadnought*-type ships, other countries, particularly Germany, tried to keep pace, provoking an arms race. The Admiralty were particularly concerned that German shipyards, by 1909, would have developed the capacity to build greater numbers of more powerful ships than could Britain.

Each side attempted to keep itself informed about the plans of the other, and it was for this reason that both countries employed spies, whilst ostensibly trying to find a diplomatic solution to their rivalry, before war or bankruptcy intervened. German demands always exceeded what Britain was prepared to concede: Germany wished to detach Britain from her alliance with France and from friendly relations with Russia. A system for the mutual exchange of information on naval building programmes, agreed between Britain and Germany, and intended to counter the worst effects of the arms race, was rendered null and void because of German insistence that Britain should not amend her own naval programme in the light of the information which it received from the Germans.

Information concerning German intentions and technologies had, therefore, to be obtained by other, more clandestine, means. The whole situation was exacerbated in the mind of the British public by a series of novels and plays, particularly those of the author William Le Queux. His books, of which the best known was *Spies of the Kaiser* (published in 1909), imagined a German invasion of Britain, aided by an army of 6,500 spies who were 'known' to be in this country, with a cache of 60,000 rifles 'known' to be hidden in a basement near Charing Cross, who were just waiting for 'Der Tag', the day when they would rise up in support of a German invasion and paralyse the capital. The Government, these books alleged, knew about the spies, but chose to do nothing. It was left to Le Queux to expose this menace, so he stalked the lanes of Surrey at night with a flashlight and revolver, searching for the enemy. He was aided and abetted in his self-imposed task by elements of the popular press, such as the *Weekly News*, which ran a spy-spotting competition for its readers, or another journal that appointed a special Spy Editor. The fact that no trace of these spies was ever found served only to prove to Le Queux and his allies the extent of the Germans' cunning.

Although Britain considered Germany its most serious threat, the adoption of the 'two power standard' meant that other navies had to be watched as well. In 1909, just as the potential of German shipyards was about to be realised, both Italy and Austria announced the start of their own battleship-building programmes. Not only were these two countries allies of Germany, but their naval power was based in the Mediterranean, and so formed a potential threat to communications between Britain and India. The Government of the day, under the Liberal Prime Minister Campbell-Bannerman, had come to power on a platform that included reducing armaments spending to finance social programmes, such as the introduction of National Insurance. This sudden new threat provoked a serious split within the Cabinet, between those who favoured the strongest possible Navy, led by the First Lord of the Admiralty, Winston Churchill, and those who wanted to reduce armaments spending, led by David Lloyd George. The Churchillian faction won the day; the result of this 'Naval Scare' and the controversy it provoked resulted in the continued, even accelerated, construction of battleships for the Royal Navy.

It would have come as something of shock to the German authorities, and even to some members of the British establishment, to learn that there was in fact *no* intelligence-gathering organisation within the British Government to operate any kind of espionage network, either against the Germans or indeed any other foreign power. The existing Naval and Military Intelligence Departments, both formed in the early 1880s, had been allowed to decline into desuetude with no voices raised in protest. The feeling shared by successive governments of the nineteenth century was that the Royal Navy would act as sufficient safeguard against any attack by a major power; accordingly, there was no need to spend money on intelligence-gathering operations. The Naval Scare of 1909 changed everything, bringing home to the Government just how suddenly the international situation could change and how little they knew about the real intentions and capabilities of foreign countries. In the October of that year, therefore, it was decided forthwith to set up a foreign section within the Secret Service Bureau, itself set up only months before.

The head of the new foreign section was Commander (later Captain Sir) Mansfield George Smith Cumming R.N. He was known within the section simply as 'C', a code name still in use to-day for the Head of M.I.6. According to the writer Compton Mackenzie, who met him in 1916 (and went on to work for Cumming in Greece during the First World War), this naval officer was 'a pale clean-shaven man, the most striking features of whose face was [*sic*] a Punch-like chin, a small and beautifully fine bow of a mouth and a pair of very bright eyes', which glared out at the world through a gold-rimmed monocle. Although by then middle-aged (he was born in 1859), he delighted in yachts, fast cars and aircraft, and during the First World War was noted for driving his Rolls-Royce around London at breakneck speeds, much to the despair of the police. Although he could speak not a word of German, this did not prevent him from conducting several spying missions on his own: he regarded it all as 'capital sport'.

Having created the section, the Cabinet demanded up-to-date, accurate information about German intentions and capabilities. Yet, at the same time, it failed to allocate a budget sufficient to the task. Cumming was given no time to set up a permanent network of trained agents, and was forced to rely on so-called 'casual agents', men who were by no means professionals in intelligence work, but simply reliable people who could report back whatever information they could acquire. There seems little doubt that Cumming recruited men whom he thought shared a similar outlook on life. John Herbert-Spottiswoode, for example, was a member of the Royal Aero Club at the same time as Cumming.

Spottiswoode had been a test pilot for A.V. Roe's aircraft company, and had seen thirty-nine of his friends killed in aircraft accidents within two years. Anxious to find another line of work, and heavily in debt, Spottiswoode agreed to Cumming's suggestion that he pose as an Irish-

American in Germany, and use his fluent German and his aviation experience to try and obtain information about Zeppelin construction. After the war, Spottiswoode claimed to have even worked in a Zeppelin factory, using his alleged American nationality to stay on in Germany after 1914; but he was man with a nervous disposition, and never looked back on his time as a spy with any fondness.

Given the rather haphazard method of recruitment, it is scarcely surprising that not everyone recruited by 'C' was a success. Cumming's best spy – certainly his most famous – was the man born Sigmund Georgevich Rosenblum, more celebrated under his adopted name of Sidney Reilly. Reilly's career is obscure in many of its details, not least because Reilly himself told several tall and contradictory tales designed to impress or confuse about his life as a spy, both before and during the First World War, and later in revolutionary Russia. It does seem possible, however, that from around 1911 he worked as the St. Petersburg agent for the German shipbuilding concern of Blohm und Voss of Hamburg, and was thus able to make copies of all their new developments.

But few of Cumming's agents were as successful as Reilly, partly because they were untrained, and partly because the Admiralty and the War Office continued to despatch their own agents to Germany in addition to anyone that he might send. One of the Admiralty's forays involved Lieutenant Vivien Brandon, R.N. of the Admiralty Hydrographic Department (the Navy's map makers) and Captain Bernard Trench of the Royal Marines, who were sent to reconnoitre German defences on the North Sea coast in 1910. Both were quickly arrested, and a large number of incriminating documents were found with them. At the time of their arrest, they not only admitted to having entered the fortifications at Borkum (something of which their interrogators were completely unaware), but also confessed to sending regular telegraphs to someone called 'Reggie' in the Naval Intelligence Department in London. 'Reggie' was the Assistant Director of Naval Intelligence, Captain Roy Regnart, another Royal Marines officer. Both Brandon and Trench received sentences of four years' imprisonment.

Another of these part-time agents was one Bertrand Stewart. He had first approached the War Office in 1911; they passed him on to Cumming. Stewart did not have a clue about spying, other than what he had gathered from the pages of the novels of William Le Queux, but expressed the desire to do 'something spectacular in the way of discovering German preparations for the war'. At the insistence of the War Office, and against Cumming's better judgement, Stewart was sent to Germany, only to be taken in by a double agent, and quickly arrested and imprisoned. The ease with which these amateur agents were captured only served to make the German authorities anxious to be on the look-out for more. The lack of co-ordination between the various British departments led to confusion and duplication.

Before taking up his duties in Intelligence, Cumming had been the commander of the Southampton port boom defences, from offices in an old warship, H.M.S. *Argo*. When not on duty, he was frequently to be found sailing on the Solent, since he lived on a houseboat at Burlesdon, as well as owning a large number of boats at one time or another, including three motor launches (the *Comely*, *Commandant* and *Communicator*), a 'luxurious' ten-ton yacht (the schooner *Barbara*), and several sailing dinghies; he was also a member of the Royal Southern Yacht Club and the Motor Yacht Club, which were both involved in holding races during Cowes Week. Given that Max's business was now based in Southampton, it seems more than likely that the two first met in Solent yachting circles.

In an account of Naval intelligence written in 1931, a former agent, Hector Bywater, comments that it was difficult to find agents who had the technical knowledge to perform their duties satisfactorily, to sort the genuine information from the useless. The best cover, he declared, was a legitimate business. Further, any potential agent needed a command of German, to be a good social mixer, and to have steady nerves. All of which Max had in abundance.

Max is supposed to have offered an alternative explanation. Alan Judd, in his biography of Cumming, quotes an incident from the latter's diary. Cumming had interviewed a potential agent, referred to only by the code name of Ironmoulder. Ironmoulder knew Max, and must have been aware that Max knew Cumming, since he had tried to pump Max for everything he knew about 'C'. In the course of the conversation, Max revealed to Ironmoulder that Cumming carried a warrant in his pocket for Max's arrest. What an extraordinary and indiscreet thing for Max to say. Perhaps Max himself was trying to recruit Ironmoulder for Secret Service work: work which, at the time, was not the sort of thing a 'gentlemen' would do. Max could, therefore, have been trying to show that he was only engaged in such work by dint of compulsion by Cumming. Of the various agents whom Cumming recruited, and who are mentioned by Judd, none appear to have been coerced into the work – all joined either from a sense of patriotic duty (mostly serving officers), or for money. In his own account, Max certainly does not mention any hold that Cumming might have had over him.

Whatever the reason behind Max's recruitment, he may have been passing information to Cumming almost from the beginning in 1909. The Germans were later to conclude that Max's career had begun with the Ostend Regatta of 1910. If this is correct, then his presence in the Mediterranean in 1909 – the year of the 'Naval Scare' about the proposed size of the Italian fleet – can be only co-incidence. It is tempting to conclude, however, that Max had hoped to accomplish something here as well. Yet his main role for Cumming was not to gather intelligence itself, but rather to put himself into contact with men who had specialist first-hand knowledge, and then introduce them to Cumming or one of his men.

Max went to Germany in August 1910, he could still speak some German, and could follow it as well, if it was spoken slowly enough. His first contact was a man named Ernst von Maack, aged 60, who was later described as a businessman. Max asked him if he would be willing to correspond with some of his English friends 'who were interested in naval matters'. The German agreed; he was able to give Max information about proposals to make use of the merchant ships of Nord-Deutsche Lloyd and the Hamburg-Amerika Line during wartime. The Admiralty were worried, rightly as it turned out, about the possibility that these ships might be armed in wartime, and thus be able to carry out raids on British merchant ships. Maack also promised to give him details of a ship's motor made by a company in southern Germany. While Max was in Germany, Maack's landlady, Frau Ida Eckermann, introduced Max to two naval engineers, Karl Hipsich and Bernhardt Wulff, who also lodged with her.

Wulff, aged 34, had worked for the Norddeutsche Maschinen und Armaturen Fabrik in Bremen for six years, and was engaged on research in underwater signalling, both between ships and between ships and submarines. His company was also part of a syndicate that was trying to secure the contract to build the engines for the next generation of German battleships.

Hipsich worked at the Weser Werft shipyards, also in Bremen, and had been employed there for twelve years. He was an Austrian by birth (co-incidentally, he had been born in the same year as Wulff, 1877), but had changed nationalities in 1909, in response to a new regulation that only German subjects could work in German naval yards. He had made a collection of plans and notes in the course of his work in the draughtsmen's office. This information was readily to hand and was so impressive that Max arranged for him to come over to England in January 1911, bringing his collection with him.

Hipsich's own interests lay not in marine engineering but in aeronautics. He had designed a new type of aircraft that he thought would be revolutionary. When Hipsich made his trip to England, Max arranged, through Cumming, for him to meet a Mr. G.W. who might be interested in developing the design. 'G.W.' was almost certainly Montague Grahame White, another of Cumming's personal friends, and the owner of an aircraft manufacturing company. However, 'G.W.' rejected the design on the grounds of its impracticability – the proposed machine was to be 200 metres long, armed with fifty cannon, manned by a crew of nearly one hundred, and was armoured by half a metre of steel (and such a monster would still be impractical to-day!). Grahame White's rejection of Hipsich's design is rather ironic, considering that when his own company designed aircraft for the Royal Flying Corps during World War One, they, too, were rejected in favour of other, more practical types.

Hipsich was visibly disappointed at this rejection. So, to cheer him up, Max and Cumming took him to Hendon aerodrome(the home of the Royal Aero Club, where Cumming was a member), where he was allowed to examine some of the aircraft parked there. Hipsich was so pleased with the unexpected visit that, according to Cumming, 'he threw his arms around Max's neck and kissed him loudly on both cheeks'. He was quite prepared to repeat the performance with Cumming, but the latter managed to elude the German's approaches. Hipsich asked what he could do to repay the kindness they had shown him. Now came the sting in the tail: Max suggested that he should give Cumming some information about the naval designs on which he was working at the time. A deal was struck.

Hipsich was interviewed as 12 Park Place, St. James's, London, the following day. It quickly became apparent that both the scope and amount of his information was greater than Cumming had anticipated. He sent for 'Reggie' Regnart, who arrived with plans and a list of more detailed questions. The interview lasted some four hours. Cumming was exceptionally pleased by the quality of the information which Hipsich supplied: 'more than we have collected during the previous year from all the other agents put together . . . we have . . . for the first time . . . more than value for money' he later confided to his diary. Cumming agreed to give Hipsich an advance of 400 Marks, plus a further 80 Marks a month as a retainer for supplying further information (£20 and £4 at the time, the equivalent of roughly £625 and £125 respectively at current prices). Cumming also requested that Max be paid a permanent salary as a reward for finding Hipsich: he had 'well earned it.' Hipsich spent a second day at Hendon before returning to Germany. But it would seem that the German Political Police already suspected him, and from the time Hipsich returned to Germany he was followed.

On his arrival in this country, Hipsich had brought with him a lady friend, not named by Cumming. In his biography of Cumming, Judd concludes that it was Frau Eckermann, the 27-year-old Hamburg landlady who had introduced Hipsich to Max, but this is by no means certain. Whoever she was, Cumming distrusted her instinctively. He later recorded, 'As for keeping him [i.e. Hipsich] clear of the woman, his friends Wulff and Maack, and Max S, this will be almost impossible

. . . no one can control the woman or her partner Wulff. At first her demands will stimulate H[ipsich], but as she becomes more greedy, he will find himself hard put to keep pace with them and will either quarrel with her or get caught trying to do too much.' Prophetic words indeed.

Although he did not realise it, Max had also come under suspicion. On a previous visit to Germany in November or December 1910, he had gone to Hamburg to meet a Dane named Neilsen, who was acting as an agent for a Captain Robertson (Max does not explain who Robertson was – presumably he was an officer employed either at a British Embassy, or in one of the various intelligence departments in London). Neilsen had been provided with some special kind of camera by the British, but the results of his photography had not come up to expectations. Max was told to get into contact with Neilsen, and try and see what the problem was. They met at a café one evening, where Neilsen tried to get Max a little drunk. Neilsen started to complain about £10 which was still owed to him, he claimed, for previous work done; then he pulled out some plans which he tried to sell to Max there and then. Sensing some kind of trap, Max refused point blank and told Neilsen to stop talking nonsense. That put an end to the evening, and Max returned to England, where he tried to convince his superiors that Neilsen was perhaps a little unstable, and certainly not to be trusted. Max was correct, for Neilsen was a double agent, and worked for the Political Police in Hamburg.

4
ARREST AND TRIAL

Max returned to Germany once more at the beginning of March 1911. He states that his mission was to discover as much as he could about the new German dreadnought *Thüringen* (then completing at the Weser Yards in Bremen), the new battle-cruiser *Moltke* (completed at the Blohm und Voss Yards at Hamburg in October 1911), and the new German submarines. Max referred to them by the none-too-subtle codename of 'little fishes' – the first German submarine, built in Kiel in 1906, had been called the *Karp*. A newspaper report of his trial reveals that he was also interested in a new battleship with the yard name *Ersatz Odin* (renamed *Prinzregent Luitpold* on her completion at Kiel in 1913). His cover was, as usual, the buying and selling of yachts – indeed, he had just sold a yacht named the *Hiawatha* to two officers of the German Navy. On arriving in Hamburg, Max wired Hipsich and Wulff to come and meet him at his hotel 'quite late at night'. He briefed them on the information that he was looking for, then the two Germans returned home, Hipsich to Bremen and Wulff to Kiel. All three arranged to meet in Hamburg once more the following Monday.

One of the German ships about which Max was seeking information: the battleship Thüringen.

By the time Monday evening arrived, there had been no word from Wulff, and Max was a little concerned. Then Hipsich turned up, but with him was his woman friend (who Max discreetly and gallantly refers to as Madame X) and some other, male, friends whom Max does not name. Was this women indeed Frau Eckermann? In Max's own account of his time in Germany he always refers to Eckermann by name; why should he suddenly become coy, and refer to her here as Madame X if the two were one and the same?

They all went on to a nearby café. Max was startled by the presence of the newcomers, and was unwilling to trust them on first acquaintance. He tried to warn Hipsich to be careful, but the German took no notice, and proceeded to produce a set of naval plans under cover of a large tourist map of Hamburg, right in the middle of the café!

Despite his shock at this turn of events, Max managed to conceal the plans temporarily, by making a big show of folding up the tourist map and putting it in his briefcase. He then asked a waiter to put the case away for safekeeping. The men who had accompanied Hipsich and Madame X tried without success to make a grab for the bag, which Max had placed behind the bar, and, whilst all this was going on, he managed to slip the naval plans into the pocket of his overcoat.

Max soon announced that it was time to go, as Madame X had to catch the next train for Bremen, and so they all made their way towards the station. An argument developed, and, while everyone was distracted, Max was able to seal the plans in an envelope, and post them at the large brass post-box on Hamburg station. He managed to

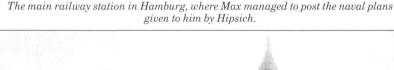

The main railway station in Hamburg, where Max managed to post the naval plans given to him by Hipsich.

arrange with Hipsich to meet again on Wednesday; then, after seeing Hipsich and his party safely off to Bremen, he was able to return to the cafe and retrieve his briefcase.

Max waited anxiously in his hotel for news of Hipsich and Wulff. Wulff turned up the next day, and Max arranged to see him again on Wednesday, with Hipsich. But neither man put in an appearance. Max wired them, 'Why don't you come down?', but for two days there was no reply. Max was by now becoming extremely concerned. He got in touch with London to check that his package had been received safely – it contained plans of the *Thüringen*, information about the *Moltke*, and details of a new German 35cm-calibre naval gun. But now there was some kind of break-down in communication, with results that proved fatal to Max's mission. Max wired, 'Have you received the £500?', meaning, 'Have you received the packet addressed to P.O. Box 500?', the address used by Cumming's Section (which also hid behind the cover of a company, Rasen Falcon & Co., Shippers and Exporters). But the telegram was either received, or was read, as saying, 'Have you received £500?', omitting the word 'the'. The wording of the telegram now implied, 'What was the value of the information contained in the packet?'. London replied, 'Things not worth £500. Only worth £10'. This revealed that something of value had been passed by Hipsich to Max, and, as the telegram was intercepted by the Political Police, it became part of the evidence that would help convict them all.

By Friday, all three men suspected that they were in serious trouble. Both Hipsich and Wulff now knew they were being followed – Hipsich had spotted his tail at the railway station thanks to a friendly ticket-collector – and were sending Max telegrams which read, 'Beware of trouble. Am being followed' (equally damning if they had been intercepted). Max decided to wait no longer for another meeting with his two sources, and made up his mind to leave Germany, probably for Rotterdam, and perhaps wait there until the heat died down. But, having intercepted his telegrams and some letters, the Police were able to outguess him. As he was leaving his hotel on Saturday, four policemen arrested him in the street, putting him into a police car, and taking him to the police station in the Town Hall.

On arrival at the Town Hall, Max's interrogation began. His inquisitors included not only the local Political Police, but also a Captain Tapkin of the German Naval Intelligence Department. Max's pockets were emptied and the police began to smoke his cigars. Max did not allow himself to be discomforted by this, and coolly began to smoke one himself. He continued to play the affable Englishman throughout, buying his interrogators a round of drinks in the police canteen. The only evidence that the police seemed to have against

Another of the German ships, the battlecruiser Moltke.

The Town Hall in Hamburg, where Max was taken after he was arrested.

A third vessel, the battleship Prinzregent Luitpold, *the former* Ersatz Odin.

Max were the intercepted letters and telegrams; although perhaps incriminating, these were not conclusive proof of his guilt, so Max continued to brazen it out. The initial interrogation lasted until 4 a.m. on Sunday morning. He was then taken away to prison, only to be returned to the Town Hall four hours later.

On his way into the interview room, he saw (or was allowed to see by his captors) Frau Eckermann, Hipsich and Maack, all in custody. He realised that his ring of contacts had all been scooped up and that he might be in more serious trouble than he had previously realised. Knowing that he had to concoct some kind of cover story, he proceeded to do so, blending provable facts with unprovable ones. His story was that, whilst at the 1910 Ostend Regatta, he had met with a lady and her two gentlemen companions, with a view to selling her a yacht. It was this woman who was Hipsich's main contact, and it was she who had taken him to England in January so that he could sell the plans of a revolutionary new aeroplane. At first Max would not reveal the woman's name, stating that he would rather hang; but then he deliberately let slip the name Lady Mabel Belmont, adding hastily to his interrogators, 'I beg your pardon, I have given it away, but don't mention it against me.' His interrogators immediately gave him books of photographs to identify this woman. He also began by refusing to name Lady Mabel's two companions, but then picked two names at random – a Captain Currie and a Major Bernstein – from a similar book of male political offenders.

Some of this could be proved. He had indeed met a woman at Ostend in 1910, and she had been seen in the company of at least one other man. Max had not only met her on board the *Lady Esmerelda*, but also at other social occasions on shore. But she was no more than one of Max's circle of social acquaintances, and had nothing to do with Intelligence. Yet Max managed to convince his interrogators that Lady Mabel Belmont was his main contact within the British Secret Service, and that his own role was quite minor. According to Max, the German police continued trying to trace her until 1918, but, since she was simply a figment of Max's imagination, it is no surprise that all their attempts proved fruitless.

Having concocted this story, Max was concerned to keep London informed, so that they might produce some incident or document in corroboration. Returned to prison, he began to make enquiries from other prisoners to see if it were possible to smuggle out a letter behind the backs of the police or the prison authorities. He learned that it was indeed possible to do so, and wrote two innocuous letters to test the system. When there were no repercussions, he sent a third to 'C', giving brief details of his fate and of the story he had fabricated. This started a brief exchange of letters with London, with, surprisingly, no real checks taking place on their contents. Whilst Max was pleased to have informed London of his actions, he glumly commented, 'never even got a thank you for it from H.Q.'

Max's interrogation continued for nine long months; during this time he was examined and re-examined, and nearly everyone who had ever spoken to him – some twenty or thirty people, according to Max – was brought in for questioning. He made two attempts at escape. His first try, in the company of another prisoner, took advantage of the building work associated with the construction of an underground railway in the city: scaling a wall, his companion managed to get away, but Max was discovered by the guards. On the second occasion, Max was just climbing over the top of the wall of the Stadthaus (the Town Hall) when armed guards appeared and apprehended him.

His trial did not begin until 7 November 1911, before the main Imperial Criminal Court in Leipzig, on the other side of Germany, many miles distant from Hamburg. Max was represented by a Dr. Süpfle, with another lawyer, a Dr. Breymann, acting as interpreter. Süpfle told Max that he was in a very grave situation, and that there was a possibility he could be put against a wall and shot. However, if Max were to reveal the names of his accomplices, then things might go easier for him. Max refused. All five defendants (Max, Hipsich, Wulff,

The Imperial Court in Leipzig, where Max was tried.

Eckermann and Maack) were charged with bringing 'to the attention of the "English Information Department" plans, drawings and other articles which ought to be kept secret in the interests of the German Empire, in contravention of paragraph 1 of the Law of July 3rd 1893, regarding the betrayal of military secrets, together with paragraph 47 of the Imperial Penal Code'. In addition Hipsich was also charged with breaches of the law of copyright (presumably on plans he may have copied from others). Once the charges had been read, the State Prosecutor, Dr. Schweigger, requested that the public should be excluded from the trial on the grounds that it would touch on matters which, if discussed publicly, would endanger the Empire. After a brief discussion, his request was granted.

Although the hearing was held in camera, it is possible to reconstruct some of the events at the trial thanks to newspaper reports, the reports of the British Consul in Leipzig, and letters and documents in Max's prison record. Some twenty witnesses were called, including people who themselves were under suspicion of involvement in the spy-ring. A number of expert witnesses also took part in the trial, including two high-ranking naval officers and a senior civil servant from naval construction (*Geheimer Oberbaurat* Pöhlmann). More information was revealed by a series of leaks, which can only have been officially inspired, and which appeared in the Leipzig newspapers. The tactics of Max's defence team seemed to be to dispute every small discrepancy in the evidence. This did not perturb the newspapers. When Max was arrested, one of his captors remarked that he had been unlucky to be caught; Max allegedly replied, 'Oh no, it was lucky for me, because if I had not been arrested, I should have done a great deal more, and I would not have got out of Germany again in less than twenty years.' This 'confession' did away with much of the argument over his guilt. But what concerned the newspapers most was that Schultz and his ring were controlled by 'various higher placed English agents . . . even well situated persons, out of the best circles in England, take part in this "patriotic service"'.

To some extent this was true, since most of the British spies apprehended by the Germans were either serving officers or men with some kind of military experience – such as Lieutenant Brandon and Captain Trench, or the hapless Bertrand Stewart (who had been an officer in the yeomanry) – or were men drawn from that same strata of society, such as John Herbert-Spottiswoode. But could the piece also have been referring, if only obliquely, to 'Lady Mabel Belmont'?

What was Max's intention in making this confession? Rear Admiral Bethell, the Director of Naval Intelligence, commented to Cumming that, 'Max is past praying for I should say he has helped very materially to get himself a long sentence – he must be mad I think.' It is possible he wished to bring the case to a premature conclusion by his confession, and so prevent the German police making further enquiries which might reveal other agents or accomplices. On the other hand, he had been promised a shorter sentence by Tapkin and the State Prosecutor if he confessed and named all his contacts; if he thought he could fend them off with the Belmont story then little had been lost. Yet his confession had certainly sealed his fate, and that of the others.

The reports which appeared in the German newspapers were regarded with distaste in London, since, under English law, they constituted a contempt of court. Reading the translated extract sent in a dispatch from the British Consul, one Foreign Office official commented that the report 'was most objectionable', and feared 'the leakage must have a deliberate object', but concluded that there was little that could be done by the Government. Another official was to comment later that, 'Mr. Pecksniff was a model of noble simplicity and ingenuousness compared with the writers and inspirers of the German press'.

Hipsich tried to deny any involvement with spying. He had, he said, gone to London to look up Max simply in connection with a patent connected to his aeroplane design; the money he had been given (the 400 Marks advanced to him by Cumming) was merely travelling expenses. Naturally, he said, it was no wonder that he and Max should talk about ships, since that was what they had in common. Max, he claimed, had exploited him; Max had only to tell the 'truth' at the trial, and he, Hipsich, could be set free immediately. As late as 1917, his lawyers continued to press for Max to be interrogated again with a view to retracting his testimony, claiming that Hipsich had been convicted on Max's testimony alone. However, as the prosecution stated at the time of the trial, this ignores the fact that Hipsich undoubtedly passed plans that were clearly stamped 'Secret' to Max, and perhaps direct to London as well. But the unfortunate Hipsich was unsuccessful in his attempts to have the case reopened, and still protesting, disappears from our story.

Frau Eckermann also denied any involvement in spying, and continued to do so even after her sentence was pronounced, shouting her innocence from the dock. Indeed, it does seem likely that she was telling the truth and that her only offence had been to introduce the guilty men to each other.

The trial lasted three days, and all five defendants were eventually found guilty. Max was sentenced to seven years' penal servitude with a further ten years' loss of civil rights; his release was laid down most precisely as 13 June 1918, at ten minutes past two in the afternoon. Of the others, Hipsich was given twelve years' imprisonment and ten years' loss of civil rights; Wulff received two years in prison and five years' loss of rights; whilst both Eckermann and von Maack received three years' prison and five years' loss of civil rights. Hipsich was found the 'most' guilty, since, as a State employee, it was deemed that he had full knowledge of the implications of what he was doing. In contrast, Schultz received more lenient treatment because he was a foreigner, and also because his prosecutors could not prove the full extent of his involvement. The offences of Eckermann and von Maack were of a lesser degree, which, therefore, merited shorter sentences, and, whilst it could not be proved that Wulff had actually passed any information over to Schultz, he was certainly found guilty of an intent to do so.

Max was taken from Leipzig to the jail for political prisoners at Brandenburg about forty miles south of Berlin. He joined a prison community of 'about fifty or sixty so-called spies, mostly Germans and Jews'. The officials of this prison, he recalled, were so brutal that the warders had to look towards the prisoners for sympathy. The regime had become even harsher after the escape of a French spy, a Captain Lux, from a prison elsewhere in Germany just before Max went to trial; after this, the prisoners found themselves under constant observation, day and night. Max spent two months there before being moved to another prison, at Zonenburg, which was also in Prussia, some thirty miles north of Berlin. This was a seventeenth-century nobleman's palace, built in the baroque style, and since converted into a jail. But Max was not to spend long there, either. The Hamburg Political Police intervened and had Max transferred to Fuhlsbüttel prison on the outskirts of that city, hoping that, by treating Max leniently, he would tell them more about the elusive Lady Mabel Belmont. Accompanied by two warders, then, wearing prison clothing and in chains, Max was taken by train, first to Cüstrin-Berlin station, and then to Hamburg.

A British Foreign Office official, taking a wider view of the trial, noted that Max's capture and trial had occurred at an 'unfortunate time', for, whilst he was under arrest, the Agadir Crisis had broken, and tensions increased between Germany on the one hand, and France and Great Britain on the other. On 1 July, the German gunboat *Panther* had entered Moroccan waters, ostensibly to protect German interests within the small German enclave at the Atlantic port of Agadir, at a time of widespread civil unrest in the country. However, behind that gesture was a calculated insult aimed at the French, who claimed a protectorate over Morocco and would not brook any interference within their sphere of influence. Britain became involved in support of her ally, France. Attempts to resolve the crisis were coming to fruition just as Max had fallen into German hands. To make matters worse, the solution agreed upon largely favoured France; in return for a little territory in West Africa, Germany was forced into a humiliating climb down.

The Agadir Crisis and the apparently endless round of spy scares which afflicted Germany at this time – involving not only British spies, but French and Russians as well – contributed to a feeling of international isolation, and a sense of hostility towards her 'enemies'. Whilst not a direct cause of the war which broke out in 1914, it certainly contributed to the kind of heated atmosphere which made war more likely.

The Times first reported Max's arrest on 20 March, quoting German newspaper reports that an Englishman and several Germans had been taken into custody. Max was not actually named by the newspaper until the 24th. But it is a measure of how successful Max had been in keeping this side of his life secret that the first thing the family knew of his arrest was a headline in the *Daily Mirror* – 'Britain's greatest spy captured', complete with pictures of Max and a two-page spread on the story. The Official Secrets Act had only just come into law in 1911 – the newspaper's editor obviously was not going to let it come between him and a good story!

5

IN PRISON

The jail at Fuhlsbüttel was Hamburg's political prison. It was deliberately sited amidst the green fields to the north of the city, to allow the criminals who were sent there to reflect on and repent of their wicked ways in 'idyllic' surroundings. During the Second World War, it became a concentration camp and a Gestapo prison. Still a jail to-day, it is now surrounded by Hamburg's northern suburbs. Once he had arrived there from Zonenburg and passed through its turreted gateway with its prominent coat of arms, Max was immediately placed in solitary confinement, in a cell on one of the prison's north-facing wings. He was rarely alone for long, however, for, in addition to the regular surveillance of prison staff, he also had several visitors. One of these was the local Inspector from the Political Police, Drössler by name, curious about this English spy. 'I was made a great fuss of by the Inspector of Police,' Max recalled. 'He was always in my cell and wanting to know . . . about secret systems of writing.' That apparently had not formed any part of Max's training in intelligence work, for he claimed everything he told the Inspector about secret writing came from the pages of Charles Dickens. Even so, it was sufficient to impress the policeman; but there was an ulterior motive behind these apparently friendly visits. One day a warden said to Max, 'Herr Dresser [sic] of the Political Police has been here and asked me to look after you, and he promised me a medal if I could get anything out of you.'

Max replied, 'If I can assist you in getting that medal, I shall do so.'

The only help that Max could possibly give Inspector Drössler and his colleagues was to reveal to them the names of other British agents. This he refused to do. Nevertheless, he claimed that by appearing to be a little co-operative, he kept them hanging on for three years, hoping that he might one day crack, and reveal all. The one benefit from the Inspector's visits was that, since he appeared to be a favoured prisoner of the Political Police, he was saved from the attentions of the 'crotchety' warders. Conditions were otherwise reasonable, Max recalled, with very good food indeed. The prison itself, as he commented in a letter to Sarah, was only 'a decent cab drive' from the centre of Hamburg, which would make visiting easier, for there was already a direct steamship route from Hull. Max was certainly glad to be away from the grim Prussian gaols.

The Political Police formed a special branch of the Hamburg Police, responsible for rooting out the political dissent that was felt to threaten the existence of the Imperial State. But the Hamburg force had not always included such a political element of this kind. For most of the second half of the nineteenth century, it had been very British in outlook and even in appearance – its policemen wore a uniform which was very British in style and were known by the British ranks of *Constabler* and *Sergeant*. This all changed in 1892, in the wake of German unification: as part of a process of remodelling all the different German police forces along Prussian lines – the constables were now called *Schütze*, the sergeants *Wachtmeister*, and the uniform was changed to include the spiked helmet, the *pickelhaube*. The Political Police were introduced into the Hamburg force at the same time. One of the first duties of the newly-created section was to send spies, dressed in ordinary civilian clothes, into cafés and bars, to listen in on private conversations, and to note down the names of those who held 'subversive' opinions. The most outspoken of the latter soon found themselves in Fuhlsbüttel prison.

The police continued to take an interest in Max whilst he was in prison, interrogating their captive several times more in the hope of obtaining the names of others among his contacts. In a statement made in 1916, Max claims that he was a witness in a number of cases, one in Essen in January 1912, and three in Hamburg during the following year. He does not say whether he acted for the defence or the prosecution, but it would seem that in each case he acted for the State. However, because the trials were held in camera, it is impossible to say what evidence, if any, he was able to provide.

Max was always kept separate from his fellow prisoners, and given better work than the others – he was employed in making cigars for much of the time. Alone in his cell, he also found some spare time to make his ship models, the *Imperator* included. The ship, which so attracted Herr Knölke some eighty or so years later, was formed from a solid piece of beech wood, one metre long, and carved to shape. Max then added the rails, made out of pins, and the ship's boats formed from thin lead. He does not say what provoked him into leaving his note, though from its tone he certainly appears to have reached a low ebb. Perhaps this ocean liner recalled another, the *Titanic*, which had sunk not long before. Max had known several of the officers on that ill-starred ship from his days in Southampton. The note reads:

Oct 6th 1913
To whom so ever find this may know that this is placed inside of the model of the IMPERATOR H&A Line 828 feet long, 87ft beam and 48ft depth.
    The model is built to scale by the writer in FUHLSBÜTTEL Hard Labour Prison with very odd and rough tools.
    Despise it not on account of roughness, it is a labour of love and helps to pass the time.

I am here now two and a half years, having been
sentenced in Leipzig to seven years for espionage for the
dear old English Government.

I am an English man and a ship owner residing in
Coltman Street, Hull, Yorkshire, England. Wife a Hilton
good and true, five children.

Max William Schultz

The style of the note is curious, almost as if Max was starting to
forget his English, which may well have been the case after spending
over three years in Germany – although his written memoirs,
completed after the war, show no sign of this. Max says that after two
years and nine months in Fuhlsbüttel (this would be early in 1914,
and only a few months after he had completed the model of the liner),
he made his third attempt to escape, but does not go into detail.

Sarah succeeded in visiting him on several occasions. Max
recommended that she stay at the best hotels, as representing the 'best
value on the continent', and that she should register herself by her
maiden name of Hilton, because everyone in the city would recognise
the name of Schultz. She could not speak German, so on her visits, in
April and September 1912, and again in September 1913, she was
accompanied by Max's sister Clara, who had journeyed from
Swinemünde. All the visits had to arranged in advance, and she was
obliged to seek permission from the Prison Governor before her arrival.
Sarah's first visit almost failed at this hurdle. Accompanied by her
father and by Clara, she arrived at the prison, but they were all turned
away because they could not prove their identities. They were obliged
to obtain supporting documentation from the British Consul in
Hamburg before they could visit Max – and only Sarah and Clara
managed to do so, the following day. Sarah's father managed visits of
his own, accompanied by Max's brother, in January and May 1913,
and in May 1914.

Max and his visitors could not speak English together – prison
regulations obliged a German speaker to be present at all times. The
choice usually fell on the Protestant clergyman at the prison, Pastor
Funke, who could speak sufficient English to follow a conversation
and, more importantly, to report on its contents. Neither could they
correspond in English. All letters in both directions had to be
translated into German, and, despite a protest, Max had to pay for
the translating himself, at 4 Marks per letter.

Meanwhile, Sarah was working for Max's release. Max wrote to his
father-in-law suggesting that he get in touch with two local M.P.s, Sir
Mark Sykes and Stanley Wilson, or with Wilson's cousin, the shipping
magnate Lord Nunburnholme, to see, even if they could not put

pressure on the Government of the day, at least if they could help in subsidising Sarah's visits. In May 1913, Sarah even wrote to the Kaiser, asking that Max be pardoned as an act of clemency on the double occasion of the marriage of the Kaiser's daughter, Princess Viktoria Luise, to the Duke of Brunswick-Lauenburg, and of King George V's state visit to Germany. But her efforts were in vain. The reply stated that Max was far too dangerous to Germany's security to permit his release. Not so Trench and Brandon, the two officers jailed for espionage in 1910, who were obviously thought sufficiently harmless to be released from prison at that time, seventeen months early, in an act of clemency denied to Max.

The outbreak of war with Britain on 4 August 1914 brought an abrupt change in Max's circumstances behind the walls of Fuhlsbüttel. He had contracted influenza, and was ill in bed, when the Director of the prison made an abrupt entrance into his cell. Max was ordered to strip, and was moved to another cell, the strongest in the whole complex, where every fitting was brand new, leaving no weak spots to help a potential escaper. If he was found looking out of a window, Max was warned, if he was caught speaking to anyone except the warder who opened his cell door, he would be shot. The new cell had three extra locks on the door and extra bars on the window; the slot in the door through which his food was passed was screwed tight, and, under normal circumstances, only the Head Warder was permitted to visit him.

In late 1914 Max was visited by the Director accompanied by Herr Carl Schröder, the Bürgermeister (Mayor) of Hamburg. Schröder had come to gloat, taking advantage of the presence of the only captive Englishman in that part of Germany. He told Max how many Englishmen had been killed, and how many Royal Navy battleships had been sunk. Max refused to be baited, wagering the Bürgermeister that the war would last at least three years (a remarkable prediction, considering generals on both sides were predicting a swift end to the conflict), and that Britain would be victorious at the end of it. He reminded Schröder that all the promises which had been flying around Germany on the outbreak of war – Calais captured, London in German hands within two months – remained unfulfilled. As he later recalled, there had been no mention in Germany of the Battle of the Marne, which forced the German Army to withdraw, abandoning their early gains, with Paris almost in sight.

The Head Warder also tried to needle Max when he brought in his food: 'Your friends at home won't be eating like this' was a favourite saying of his. This so infuriated Max that he once flung the tray back at the man, thus earning himself seven days' 'dark', that is, confinement in a small, unlit, punishment cell. Fortunately for Max, who was still suffering from 'flu, this order was countermanded by the prison doctor, who confined Max to bed for several months instead, giving him extensions on his confinement until the weather became milder, when he began to show signs of recovery.

Fit again, Max served his seven days' punishment. When he emerged, he was put to picking oakum just like the other prisoners, but he was still confined in his own cell. The Head Warder continued to try to provoke Max, shouting 'so many Englishmen killed' as he walked past the cell door. Even as ebullient a character as Max was beginning to feel depressed by the continual chafing. This was the period of the Battle of Neuve Chapelle and the Second Battle of Ypres, where casualties amongst British forces had indeed been heavy. Letters from home had stopped; Max had managed to smuggle out one or two, but had received nothing in reply. The Head Warder came in one day in May 1915 announcing, 'This morning I have had the finest breakfast I had in my life.'

'Oh, what is the matter?' enquired Max. 'Why have you had such a good breakfast?'

'We have blown the *Lusitania* up, and the whole crew's gone down with it,' came the chilling reply.

Max tried to make the best of it: 'That is nothing, my friend. You told me you would be in London at Christmas, and I thought you had such a good breakfast because you had heard that the Kaiser was on the throne of England.'

Max's friend, the Inspector, came to visit one last time. He had joined up, he announced, and would send Max a postcard from London. Max, refusing to buckle under, continued to maintain that the war would last three years.

If he chanced to look out of his prison window (after first ensuring, of course, that no-one was watching), Max could see the Zeppelin sheds, maintained by the German Navy, at the nearby airfield. This airfield is now Hamburg's civil airport, but before the First World War it was one of the Navy's main airship bases and was also used for civilian airship traffic. Two Zeppelins were stationed there at first, but their number was later increased to four. It was from Fuhlsbüttel that the first two Zeppelins to bomb England, L.3 and L.4, took off for the Humber ports on 19 January 1915 (and, getting lost, ended up by bombing King's Lynn and Great Yarmouth instead). Max worried every time the manoeuvring craft set off towards Wilhelmshaven or Kiel that they were going on a raid, and he began to be concerned for his family in Hull. Although it would have been but little comfort for Max, none of the Fuhlsbüttel craft were involved on the raid on Hull in June 1915 – the Zeppelin used, L.9, was at that time based at Hage, on the German North Sea coast, near the Dutch border. Indeed, hardly any further raids were mounted from Fuhlsbüttel, as newer bases were created in north-western Germany and in occupied Belgium, nearer to British targets. Amongst the other craft stationed at Fuhlsbüttel later in the war were L.6 and the Hull raider, L.9, both of which were destroyed by a fire in their hangar in September 1916 – an event that, curiously, rates no mention in Max's memoirs.

Although Fuhlsbüttel's Zeppelins played no part in the attack on Hull, the raids themselves were to have a permanent effect on Max and his family, although he know nothing of the details until the war's end. L.9, commanded by *Kapitänleutnant* Heinrich Mathy of the German Navy, emerged from a thick mist bank at around ten minutes before midnight on the night of 6 June. Quickly finding his bearings, Mathy directed the airship over Hull. First dropping parachute flares to illuminate the target, the Zeppelin followed these with five explosive and fifty incendiary bombs, opposed only by the guns of the light cruiser H.M.S. *Adventure*, then in dry dock. The bombs fell on the city in five main groups. The first bombs started a fire in the Old Town, in the very centre of the city, when they hit a large furniture store close to the medieval Holy Trinity church; a second serious fire broke out when a timber yard near Dansom Lane was hit, to the north-east of the previous explosions. Other bombs fell on and around Clarence Street and around Craven Street, on the eastern side of the city, on tightly packed areas of working-class housing, and this is where most of the casualties were sustained. The fifth area to be hit in the attack, around Walker Street, to the west of the city centre, and only about a quarter of a mile from Max's house in Coltman Street, suffered only slight damage and few casualties. Few, if any, of the bombs fell on targets of real strategic importance – the docks and railway lines, for example, remained untouched. Even so, the raid resulted in the deaths of twenty-four people, the injuring of some forty more, and in damage valued at about £44,000. The raid provoked an orgy of violence in the city; shops belonging to people with German-sounding names were ransacked, and a handful of individuals were attacked. Four such incidents of this type took place on Hessle Road, near its junction with Coltman Street. This was a little too close to home for Sarah. The raid, coming as it did not long after the *Lusitania* disaster, led to a wave of hostility towards foreigners in the city. These views were held by many people, including, it has to be said, Max's own parents-in-law, and Sarah was forced to change the family's name, adopting instead her own maiden name of Hilton.

At this time, Sarah was granted an allowance from the Government of £16 per month, and every Christmas, the family received a parcel of presents. The donor remains unknown – if Sarah knew, she did not confide in her children. One can perhaps detect the hand of Cumming here, since, although a spymaster, he was, to judge by the accounts of those who knew him when they were children, a kindly man (Bertrand Stewart's widow also received an allowance). Whoever was sending these presents certainly knew the ages of the children, for, as they grew up, the girls at least ceased to get toys and received small amounts of jewellery instead.

One of the warders at Fuhlsbüttel had a son, Carl, who was employed as a carter at the Zeppelin 'wharf' and was permitted to visit Max occasionally. From him, Max obtained much information, which, if not true to the facts, was at least indicative of the way rumours flew around in war-time Germany. According to Carl, no-one now thought highly of the Zeppelins, because they had failed to produce any lasting impact on the conduct of the war. The crews, taken straight from torpedo boats and left completely without training did not like them, and morale of the men was at absolute rock-bottom. They were so demoralised that by the time they reached their target they were physically paralysed with fear. The crew on the first Zeppelin to be shot down went insane, and, as a result, all Zeppelins were equipped with strait-jackets to restrain crew members who might go berserk. Even so, more than one crew had mutinied and killed all their officers. Over two hundred Zeppelins had been built, and over half remained unaccounted for. This last 'fact' is typically exaggerated – the German Navy, which operated most of the airships, was only ever equipped with a total of seventy-three craft, of which seventeen were lost on raids, with a total of some 389 men killed; the German Army operated an even smaller number. Far from their crews being paralysed with fright, the Zeppelins (when they succeeded in reaching their targets, for navigation was frequently difficult over the foggy North Sea) had a profound effect on the morale of British civilians, forcing the withdrawal of fighter squadrons from the Western Front back to Britain to act as a defence against the intruders.

Nevertheless, the prospect of further Zeppelin raids on England increased Max's concern about his family. After the second raid, on London, on 31 May 1915, he was anxious to send a letter out through official channels, and to this end attempted to enlist the help of the prison chaplain. Repeatedly he asked for an interview with the clergyman to plead his case, and, although he was refused several times, his requests at last met with success. After knocking on the door and entering the chaplain's office, Max was greeted by the clergyman, who exclaimed, 'Now we are moving. We are blowing all the towns to pieces. The Zeppelins are going over there. We have blown all the London docks away, and blown all the bridges down, and they have blown part of Westminster down.'

Max was not one to let such a provocative statement pass by

unchallenged, replying, 'That is very interesting. My warder's been telling me that you have blown a school up and blown a lot of children to pieces. Very interesting. And you a clergyman to take it like that.'

Having started so badly, this lively discussion continued to go downhill, ending in an argument about who was responsible for starting the war in the first place. Max left the office, to find his warder escort was nowhere in sight. As he could not wander around the prison unaccompanied, he took the provocative step of re-entering the chaplain's office, and, much to the displeasure of the occupant, demanded to be allowed to stay there until the warder turned up. Needless to say, he failed to get his letter sent out.

Max was right to be worried. His daughter Gladys had left school and was employed as a typist in an insurance office in Hull's Old Town – exactly where the Zeppelins were dropping their bombs – indeed, she was a witness to one of raids. Zeppelins paid Hull a second visit, on the night of 5/6 March 1916. In cold, snowy weather, L.14 (*Kapitänleutnant der Reserve* Aloys Böcker) emerged from cloud to find itself over Flamborough Head. It then turned south to drop a few bombs on Beverley before releasing a further twenty-one high explosive and incendiary bombs on Hull, mostly around the docks. Whilst this was happening, another airship, L.11 (*Korvettenkapitän* Viktor Schütze) arrived over the city, and succeeded in dropping some 3,600 lbs. of bombs, destroying a ship on the stocks in Earle's shipyard, blowing up water-mains and leaving a number of buildings ablaze. Both craft turned southwards with the prevailing gale force winds and made a brief attack on Killingholme before returning across the North Sea. On 5/6 April, Schütze tried to make a return visit, but the defences had improved somewhat by then, and he was driven off by anti-aircraft fire. Although several other raids came close, only one more airship succeeded in dropping bombs on Hull, on the night of 8/9 August later that same year. Ten were left dead and eleven injured – the work of L.24 (*Kapitänleutnant* Robert Koch). On this occasion, thick mist prevented the defences from offering little more than token resistance.

6
PRISON AND FREEDOM

In the middle of 1916 the course of events in the war once more forced Max on to the defensive against the taunts of his warders. The clash between the Royal Navy and the German High Seas Fleet, a clash anticipated even before Max set off on his missions to Germany, had finally taken place. On 31 May, the two fleets met in the North Sea, off the coast of Jutland. But the battle was no Trafalgar for the Royal Navy – if anything, losses of ships and men were in Germany's favour. Strategically, however, victory went to the Royal Navy, because the battle so un-nerved the German Naval Command that its still-outnumbered fleet never again ventured to sea for the rest of the war. Once news of the battle reached the prison, Max was called upon to explain how the Royal Navy, if it was indeed as powerful as everyone said, had not defeated the German Fleet. Max was not altogether sure himself, but did point out, correctly, that the Germans could only have counted the battle a victory if their fleet had broken out of the North Sea; as it was, the British blockade of Germany remained unbroken, if a little battered, and, as long as it stayed intact, then the Germans would never be in a position to win the war.

Individual warders told Max privately that they agreed with him, and beneath the show of bravado his captors seem to have taken an increasingly pessimistic view of the conflict, partly due to the long casualty lists which were being reported from the Western Front, as a result of the Battle of the Somme, and partly because of the effects of the British naval blockade. The quality of the prison food was beginning to suffer. There had never been any meat in the prison meals, and, from the middle of 1915, even things like lentils and peas began to disappear from the menu. Turnips now became the staple of the prison diet, supplemented by a few carrots and black bread. A small piece of black bread, 3½ inches square and ½ inch thick, was all there was for breakfast, washed down with 'coffee', a concoction which, if allowed to stand for any time, would clear itself into plain water and a soot-like sediment. The mid-day meal was three-quarters of a litre of turnip soup, the turnips sometimes in cubes, sometimes cooked down to a mush. At 5 o'clock the evening meal consisted of another square of black bread and some more coffee. Very occasionally, this was supplemented by fish soup, made from scraps from the Hamburg Fish Market.

But this was little different from the food available outside the prison walls. The British blockade and a bad harvest made the winter of 1916-17 a difficult one, and it became known as 'The Turnip Winter' when that humble root became the staple food of most Germans. There were rumours, which no doubt reached Max via one of the warders, that the rich were buying up all the good food; a goose could cost as much as £10 (the equivalent of £300 at to-day's prices).

Some eighteen months after his first encounter with the prison chaplain (it was now late 1916 or early 1917), Max tried once more to ask for his assistance in sending a letter home. This time, relations between the two were more cordial. The clergyman held out his hand and apologised for his previous intemperate behaviour. It became clear that the chaplain had a son in England, whether as a prisoner of war or a civilian internee, Max does not say. The chaplain was just as worried for his son as Max was for his family. This shared misfortune perhaps softened his heart towards the Englishman, and he succeeded in persuading the authorities to allow a letter through. But the reply was a trick, which must have been a devastating disappointment for Max. It apparently came from the American Consul in Hull (the American Government had volunteered to act as the representative of civilian prisoners in the two countries), who said that he had called upon Max's family, and wrote to the effect that his wife was not well and very hard up for funds. Max refused to believe this to be true, and, since he had had no direct contact with his wife, he was almost more upset than if he had heard nothing.

In October 1916, Max appealed to the Hamburg Senate for leniency in his case. He said that during his interrogation he had been promised that he would only have to serve one half of his sentence if he co-operated with the authorities. This promise had been made many times by many people including a Dr. Sieveking, the examining magistrate in his case, Captain Tapkin of German Naval Intelligence, and Police Inspector Drössler. Max had certainly been interrogated a number of times, and had, as mentioned above, given up the name of 'Lady Mabel Belmont' as well as appearing as a witness in four other cases in 1912 and 1913. Even so, it seems to have been very naïve of Max to think that, as a convicted spy, he would be released early, no matter how much he had co-operated, for he was still a citizen of a country which was at war with his captors.

Depression was rife amongst prisoners within the jail, and a growing number of inmates were committing suicide. In the cell next to Max, three or four killed themselves, and he claimed that in the first six months of 1918, the death rate in the prison rose to some fifteen or twenty per week. Max had been given the easier job of picking tobacco, rather than oakum, and was even allowed to resume work on his ship models. Then, as now, tobacco was used as currency in the prison, and Max was able to swap some with a warder for extra bread.

Max's sentence came to an end in June 1918, and he should therefore have been released. But England was still at war with Germany, and he remained an Englishman in the enemy's country. In 1914 every English man and woman living or working in Germany, but unable to return home, had been interned in a hutted camp at Ruhleben, near Berlin. By rights, as he was now no longer a criminal but an ordinary civilian internee, Max should have been transferred to Ruhleben, but this never happened. Max blamed the prison chaplain, who, he claimed, despite the personal sympathy he had shown him, had noted on a report that he still considered Max a danger to the Fatherland. Whether or not this is true is not revealed in Max's prison record, but it certainly contains a request from the Hamburg police authorities that he be placed in military detention when his prison sentence did come to a formal end on 13 June. Accordingly, he was sent to another political prison close to Hamburg, at Hütten. Hütten was then on the western outskirts of the city, but beyond the city's boundaries and in Prussian, rather than Hamburg, territory – now, like Fuhlsbüttel, the city's suburbs have grown to encompass the site. At first, conditions there were even worse than in Fuhlsbüttel. Max was once more put into solitary confinement, and given only the very minimum to eat.

However, in one respect, Max's circumstances did improve a little, since he once more began to receive letters from home, genuine this time, which contained a little money. He wrote to the prison authorities and asked to be allowed to mix with the general prison population, and even to go into town once a week to buy food. Max was granted permission to spend an hour outside the prison walls once a week or so, provided he was supervised by the Political Police. But, in practice, his excursions were limited to one a month, and then only for the first two months or so. The first thing he did was to go out and buy a meal. It came as something of a shock to him to see how badly war-time Germany was faring under the British blockade. For a menu consisting of corned beef hash with cabbage and extra potatoes, a sweet and two small glasses of white wine, he paid 27 shillings (£1.35, or about £40 at current prices), plus tip. He spent the same amount of money buying a hat.

Such prices soon exhausted his meagre supply of money. He then hit on the idea of seeing if he could obtain any funds from the Dutch Consul in Hamburg. (Since America's declaration of war in 1917, the affairs of internees, at least locally, had been looked after by the Netherlands government, although in theory they had become the responsibility of the Swiss.) He persuaded one of his detective minders to take him to see the Consul. The detective agreed, so Max immediately put pen to paper and wrote a letter in which he outlined his position: how badly he was being treated by being kept in solitary confinement, how little food he received, and how short he was of money. He asked the Consul to get in touch with some of Max's friends in England to arrange for some money to be sent to him via the Consul.

The following day, Max, accompanied by two detectives, named Peiper and Ramig, presented himself at the Dutch Consulate. Once inside the building, Max explained who he was, and asked the Consul to lend him some money. The Consul protested that he was not a money lender, but Max placed all his personal jewellery on the table, and volunteered that as security. Then, to the surprise of the detectives, he threw his letter into a pigeon-hole on the Consul's desk where they could not reach it. 'What was in that letter?' they demanded. Max assured them that it was only a request to get some money from his friends in England, but secretly he hoped that it would be his way out of Hütten.

His visit and the letter proved a success. As a result of the Dutch Consul's intervention, Max's cell was left open during the day, so that he could at least walk in the prison garden. And, from the middle of September 1918, the Consul lent Max four shillings (20p, or about £6 at current prices) a week on his jewellery. He was able finally to mix with the rest of the prisoners, and made himself useful re-learning what must have been an old skill acquired at his father's knee, by repairing around one hundred pairs of shoes for different people. The Consul continued to demand that Max be moved to Ruhleben, but Max's treatment had improved sufficiently that he no longer insisted on a transfer, and was left where he was. He was receiving letters from his wife (one containing money, so he was able to repay the Consul); he was stealing food to supplement his own ration, and perhaps just being able to talk to other prisoners must have helped improve his morale.

The inmates of Hütten were almost all communists or anti-war agitators. In 1914, a strict set of rules and regulations, the Prussian Law of Siege, was put into place throughout Germany. This restricted individual liberties and, at the same time, increased the power of local Army commanders to the point where the country was virtually a military dictatorship. The losses at the Front, the shortages caused by the blockade, and the erosion of personal liberty slowly built up a feeling of profound disenchantment with the war, and, in many, a strong desire to end it altogether. All the political parties had acquiesced in the passing of these laws, however reluctantly. This left the anti-war opposition in the hands of the radical left, who called themselves Spartacists, after Spartacus, the leader of a slave revolt against Ancient Rome. They were further inspired by the example of Russia, where the Bolsheviks had thrown out the old ruling class and withdrawn from the war entirely. There had been a big peace demonstration in Hamburg in August 1917, which came hard on the heels of a naval mutiny at Kiel in July; a bitter national strike followed in January 1918, and a local one in Hamburg in April of the same year. There was, therefore, much speculation among the rest of the prisoners about the possibility of a revolution. As an Englishman, Max's opinions on the war and on all things political were eagerly sought by his fellows, who had somehow got it into their heads that Max had been a confidant of Lloyd George, the Prime Minister – an impression he did nothing to dispel.

The strike in April had forced the Government to take precautions against any further industrial action turning into an armed revolt, and, to that end, Government officials in Hamburg were given sidearms and compelled to attend shooting practices. But the spark that set off the revolution was not in fact struck in Hamburg. On 30 October, in the naval port of Wilhelmshaven, the crews of two German battleships, one the *Thüringen*, Max's old quarry, the other her sister ship the *Helgoland*, refused to put to sea on an operation that was little more than a suicide mission against the British Fleet. Matters suddenly became very tense, and ships turned their main guns on each other, trying to coerce them into following one line or another, pro- or counter-mutiny. The German Naval Command tried to contain, and then defuse, the situation by dispersing the Fleet; only one squadron of battleships of the three in the Fleet refused to mutiny, and that was removed from the others and sent to Kiel, in the hopes of preserving discipline. However, once they had been given the opportunity to think about the actions of their comrades aboard the other ships, the men of the Kiel squadron now mutinied in their turn, asking for the release of the thousand or so matelots already in custody. Two days of discussion followed, until on 3 November, a protest march formed. The march had not gone far before it met a naval shore patrol which ordered the marchers to disperse. When they refused to obey, the patrol opened fire, leaving ten dead and twenty-nine wounded, including the commander of the patrol, who was killed by a sailor. From that point on, virtually all the sailors in the squadron revolted and disarmed their officers, raised the red flag, and took control of the port.

News of these events spread quickly throughout the country, and many incidents followed the lead set in Kiel. In an attempt to forestall such action in Hamburg, troops were called out and were temporarily garrisoned in Hütten prison. During the night of 4/5 November, the officers were in a particularly boastful mood, fuelled by good food and drink in the prison director's office, and all the talk was of turning their machine guns against anyone who approached. On the 6th, a demonstration by striking sailors was broken up by the use of gas. The following day, there was a meeting of the strikers and their sympathisers on an open area of land in the city known as the

Heiligengeistfeld. Following a number of speeches, the meeting broke up, and everyone moved off in different directions. According to Max, one group, which consisted of 'half a dozen sailors with a red handkerchief on a broom stick' advanced on Hamburg's main barracks, home of the 76th Infantry Regiment, where they were received by a ragged volley of fire from the windows. This provoked a parley on the telephone, which led to the surrender of the officers at the barracks, whilst their men joined the sailors, or at the very least stayed neutral. At about 3 o'clock in the afternoon it was the turn of the prison to come under attack. The inmates made themselves scarce, Max recalling that he got well clear of the main door, thinking that if there was going to be an assault, there would be plenty of bullets flying in that direction. Just at that moment, the main door was flung back, and in walked a grizzled-looking sailor, pistol in hand, followed by two more sailors and two or three women.

'Down with your weapons and off with your badges,' the sailor shouted, and, much to everyone's surprise and relief, the soldiers meekly complied. The officer in command was short in stature, and it was amusing, Max recalled, to see this little man trying to surrender his sword to a tall sailor.

One of the sailors, or one of their supporters, said to Max, 'What are you doing here?'

'I am a prisoner,' he replied.

'Get out,' was the response.

Max was free.

A REVOLUTION AND PEACE

Max was free – if he so wished. But the conflict was not over; he remained an Englishman on the soil of an enemy country. He could have been shot as a spy before was broke out, and would certainly be shot as a spy in time of war. So, when he was told to get out, his reply was quite simple.

'Not me,' he said.

The German said, 'We have heard about you and we might have use for you.' But he did not elaborate. Max could have a car at his disposal; they wanted, he said, 'to make an "entente cordiale" of me'. Max did not trust whatever arrangements had been put in place for him, and so remained in the jail, the last prisoner. That night he dined with the director and his staff, who felt that Max had paid them a great compliment by wanting to stay in gaol rather than leaving when he had the chance. They all spent the rest of the night gathering up the weapons and equipment left behind by the soldiers.

The following morning, the Political Police arrived at Fuhlsbüttel, and again told Max that he was free to go. Once more he refused.

'What can I do? Aren't I safer here than if I go to a hotel? I am all right here. If you will make arrangements up at Headquarters for me to go out, I can get my food out.' This was agreed, and so Max stayed in the prison for another week, until 19 November, going into the city for his meals. At the same time, the war had been halted by an Armistice, and he was anxious to get home. He asked at the Town Hall what he should do, and they got in touch with the Dutch Consul to see if there was any way he could arrange for Max to return to England.

'Tell Max I want him immediately,' said the Consul. 'There is some money for him.'

Once the two members of his police escort heard that Max had money waiting for him, they stuck to him like glue. The money had come from 'C', although Max felt that it could have come from a mysterious 'other agent' (whom Max does not name). Max also had some luck. One of the servants at the prison, a man named Wishnefsky, had achieved a position of some prominence in the city government, in the Food Control section. This Wishnefsky was anxious to keep in with Max, perhaps remembering the rumours that had flown around the prison about his supposed friendship with Lloyd George. And because Wishnefsky liked Max everyone else he met tried to stay on friendly terms with him too, to keep in with Wishnefsky and the new government.

Meanwhile, the Hamburg city council (called the Senate) had announced that it was the sole source of authority in the city, throwing off the apparatus of the Empire as soon as the Kaiser had left the country for the Netherlands on 9 November. (Although he did not officially abdicate for another three weeks, his effective authority was already at an end.) The city of Hamburg had a long tradition of independence, dating back to the days of the Hanseatic League, and had always resented the 'Prussian' attitudes of the Imperial administration (seen, for example, in the police re-organisation mentioned earlier). The men of the Senate were elected by a restricted franchise, and tended to be drawn from the wealthy businessmen of the city. In as much as they had any political philosophy at all, they stood for the improvement of Hamburg's trade, reasoning that increased trade would improve the lot of every citizen, through either profits or employment.

But, almost immediately after they made their announcement, the Senate's authority was challenged by a Workers' and Soldiers' Council, led by a man named Heise. The Council was Bolshevik-leaning, drawing its initial support from sailors and dockers. One of its first actions was to dismantle the machine-gun posts that had appeared on some street corners and to disarm the police. This was a tense moment. The machine gun posts had been set up by the Army, and no-one was sure which side the soldiers would support. All private cars were confiscated, and parked at strategic points, ready to ferry men back and forth whenever violence broke out. The police chief of Hamburg brought his family from their home into the Town Hall, where they stayed for their own safety, but the process of disarming his men went peacefully. From that point, each policeman was accompanied by a Bolshevik sailor, who maintained authority by force of arms. At the same time, the Council introduced a curfew in the city, from six o'clock at night to seven o'clock in the morning; further, no house with rooms facing on to the street was to show a light after 9 p.m. And only one week after the Workers' and Soldiers' Council had challenged the Senate, on 12 November, it declared the Senate dissolved and itself took over the government of the city.

According to a *Times* correspondent, Hamburg that November was 'a dismal sight, with its practically silent harbour, half-deserted streets, and rain-sodden bunting'. Food was very bad and very expensive; clothing and coal were scarce. There were clashes on the streets between the sailors, the so-called 'Red Guards' and groups of returning soldiers. Cars and trucks displaying the red flag, filled with armed men, hurried back and forth through the city's streets, scattering crowds of curious onlookers. One group of soldiers, from the 128th Infantry Regiment, mostly drunk, arrived in the city on their way home to East Prussia from the Front and immediately got into a series of fights, which left thirty dead and eighty-three injured. Many people welcomed the arrival of these soldiers to help control the sailors, but at the same time feared the consequences of any clash that might arise.

Although left-wing elements had been in the forefront of the revolution, the established political parties were biding their time. Once the revolution had achieved the objective of forcing the Kaiser's abdication, the mainstream parties planned to allow the radicals just a little more freedom before they turned on them and crushed them. At the same time, far right groups, such as the Vaterlands Partei, wanted to resume the war and grab swift victories to restore Germany's position in Europe; needless to say they were diametrically opposed not only to the Spartacists, who supported the Workers' and Sailors' Council, but even to more moderate centre-left parties, such as the Socialist Party (SPD) and the Independent Socialists (USPD). The attitude of soldiers returning from the Front was crucial, since they could use their training and weapons to circumvent the policies of any civilian political party. In such a large army it was possible to find all shades of political opinion, but many soldiers stood for a swift return to law and order – a stance which inevitably led to conflict with those on the Left who were trying to foment a workers' revolution.

Just as Max was preparing to go home via the Netherlands, Wishnefsky invited him for a political discussion. It seems unlikely that Max was a willing participant at first, reluctant to see his departure any further delayed, but his old instincts took over. He went along to these meetings to see what he could learn in case it could be of any benefit to the British Government. Every night, Max returned to Fuhlsbüttel with his escort of two detectives, Peiper and Ramig. In the tense, heated atmosphere of revolutionary Hamburg, no-one really trusted anyone else. The two detectives wanted to see if they could find out anything of Wishnefsky's intentions, particularly as they were worried that some old scores with the Political Police might soon be settled. Max arranged that they should spend the night in the gaol (there was, after all, plenty of room since all the prisoners had been set free).

Max picked up rumours of the counter-revolution: the Council was becoming increasingly unpopular, thanks to the influence of the returning soldiers, and fist fights between supporters of the two groups had begun to turn into gun battles. On Monday 19th, with Peiper and Ramig in attendance, Max had gone to the Dutch Consul to withdraw some of his money. The centre of the city was in uproar, and the Political Police were very worried. Apparently someone had found a 'black book' which belonged to the Inspector in charge, listing their agents and informers. Passing a group of men in the street, Max pointed to them and remarked, 'Why, there are the boys from the prison'. Ramig went white with fear: 'My God, they are going to shoot them all. Do give me your promise to protect my wife and children.'

The irony of being asked for protection by the man who had arrested him was not lost on Max. Nevertheless, he hustled the policemen into the hotel where he was now staying, put them in his room, and locked the door. The storm blew over quickly. The Political Police were merely put under arrest for a couple of hours and then released with no harm done. In the end, it seemed as if the revolutionaries just wanted to show who was in charge.

That night Max was eating in the hotel dining room when he became involved in a conversation with two men named Bettel and Norman. Over a bottle or two of wine it soon became apparent that these two were amongst the local leaders of the revolution. Max said,

'If you have any idea of this revolution you must realise it is not what you can do for me; it is what I can do for you. Now the very fact of my being here, I am the only one that can do you any good. I will bring you proof.'

The hotel manager was able to testify to Bettel and Norman that Max was well in with the Political Police at least. The following morning, Max, accompanied by his shadows Peiper and Ramig, met Bettel and Norman again. Then he dropped a little bombshell on his unsuspecting friends of the night before.

'Now you were very kind to me last night and we had a certain amount of political conversation and that kind of thing, and you offered your services as regards my passport and so on; but I brought these two men here to tell you who you were talking to. You were talking to a stranger last night. These gentlemen are from the Political Police. I am an English spy and proud of it.'

The knowledge that they had been seen in the company of a known English spy caused Bettel and Norman some concern, fearing for their position in the Government. To cover their tracks, and with the hint of a promise of some money, one of them telephoned Heise, the head, or, as *The Times* put it, the 'dictator', of the Hamburg Government.

'Heise, you must come down to-night,' he began. 'I have a man from England here, a very big man. Now then I have ordered dinner for 11 o'clock tonight. I will pay for everything. You must come down. Without this Englishman you cannot do anything.'

Max turned to Bettel and Norman, saying, 'This is a very serious thing for me. I must have my witnesses there as a representative of England. I cannot meet Mr. Heise unless I really and truly have an idea about what kind of government he is going to bring in. You know England won't recognise anything on the Russian principle ... before I [say] anything to Heise, he must answer these questions.'

What was Max's intention? He later confided in his memoirs, 'My idea was that it would be of benefit to England to protect [the new government of Hamburg] with a view to getting hold of the Kiel Canal for a certain amount of indemnity. I really had patriotic motives, and was using these revolutionists [sic] to hit Germany in the eye. If they could do anything to split up Germany as they wanted to split up Russia, I thought we ought to do it. The smaller the pieces Germany is broken into, the more difficult it would be for them to become a satisfied nation.'

Max met with Heise over the next five or six evenings, each time with a shorthand writer present to record their discussion. Meanwhile, he continued to arrange his passage home, via the Netherlands. He obtained a passport which read 'to Rotterdam and back', so that he could easily return and resume negotiations with Heise, if needs be. He took a copy of the notorious black book and notebooks with the texts of his discussions with Heise and hid them in the false bottom of a leather bag.

There was time for one last meeting with Heise. For reasons which remain obscure – perhaps he was to be a neutral witness – Max persuaded the Dutch Consul to attend. Max had promised Peiper and Ramig that he would get them across the Dutch frontier and away from the danger of reprisals, but the Consul was unwilling to grant this request, although he had nothing against Max himself leaving. The Consul was reluctant to be out on the streets after the 8.30 curfew – only a lift home in Heise's car, which had a machine gun mounted on the bonnet, would convince him to attend. The meeting broke up at 4 o'clock in the morning; by 8 o'clock, the Consul was en route for discussions with his ambassador in Berlin. Whatever conclusions the Dutch had drawn from Max's actions, they were now reluctant even to let him enter their country. Nevertheless he had his passport, and with Peiper and Ramig set off for the frontier. But the Consul was too quick, and the two Germans were prevented from entering the Netherlands by the Dutch police. Max pressed on, promising to have the two released within twenty-four hours.

He reached The Hague on 20 November. His official status was no more than that of an ex-prisoner of the Germans, and he doubted whether anyone would believe his story. He had breakfast in the American Hotel, and entering the cloakroom saw a man having his boots shined. By his appearance, and possibly by something him said, Max recognised him as an Englishman. Max approached the man, saying, 'Excuse me, are you an Englishman?'

'Yes, I am an Englishman,' was the reply.

'Well, if you are an Englishman, it's very funny to see you dodging round The Hague,' Max said. 'You must have something to do with our Legation.'

The man warned him to keep his voice down, as there were German spies everywhere. When he then admitted that he was on the Embassy staff, Max took him back to the dining room, and asked him directly,

'Do you know anything about the spy business? Can you tell me if there is a man named "C" alive?'

This amazingly indiscreet question was answered in the affirmative – 'C' was still alive, although he had lost his son and lost a leg. This rather abrupt answer concealed the tragic facts that Cumming's son, an officer in the Army, had been killed in a car accident in October 1914, somewhere behind the British Front. His father, who was travelling with him, had his leg crushed in the accident, and it was subsequently amputated (although the legend grew up that 'C' had performed the operation himself with his own penknife!).

Max asked to be escorted to the Embassy. Here he was confronted by a man in uniform who said to Max's new-found companion, 'Mr. L. you can trust him with everything.' Max does not identify either Mr. L., or the man in uniform. L was almost certainly Captain Henry Landau, a British Army officer, who had controlled one of Britain's most important spy networks in war-time Occupied Belgium; the man in uniform could well have been Landau's immediate superior, Captain Richard Tinsley, R.N.V.R., who was 'C's' 'Head of Station' in the Netherlands. Max also mentions the name of Major Lawrence Oppenheim, the Military Attaché at the British Embassy, who also ran spies for Military Intelligence.

Max passed over to these two men everything he had hidden in his bag. He then sat down and explained his story. Landau later recalled the interview in detail, and reveals what Max (whom he disguises under the surname 'Brewer') had discussed with Heise in Hamburg. It would seem that some members of the Workers' and Soldiers' Council had had enough of Prussia and the Prussianisation of Hamburg institutions that had been common before the war. They were all for declaring independence from Germany, and restoring the medieval Hanseatic League of north German cities, such as Bremen, Lübeck, Danzig and, of course, Hamburg itself. This, they knew, would be strongly resisted by Prussia, and so they were seeking at least tacit support from the British Government before making their move. They felt that this scheme would have attractions for Great Britain, not only because would it create a power friendly to Britain on the north German coast, but would also deprive Germany of most of her deep water ports, so she would never again be able to maintain a fleet of a size that would be a threat to the Royal Navy. The Council was also willing to give the British Government the large pre-war Transatlantic liner the *Vaterland* (the Government were to take the *Imperator* as war reparations – she became the Cunard liner *Berengaria*).

This was both an extraordinary and an unexpected proposal. The Workers' and Soldiers' Council was further suggesting that Max be the person to negotiate for them with the British Government. Max himself was urging speed, arguing that it was important for the British to act quickly before any opposition reaction by those opposed to the Council set in.

A car was despatched to the frontier to collect Peiper and Ramig, who were able to confirm Max's story, and present credentials from the Council. The Embassy telegraphed London to check on the identity of the new arrival and of the news which he had brought. The reply came back, 'Treat this man well. Do not let him go to Germany; let him go home at once, he deserves the best from us.' Landau states that his debriefing of Max was interrupted by the arrival of news of the Kaiser's flight into Belgium, dating their encounter to 9 November, but this must be incorrect, since, in his own account, Max is able to quote specific dates later in the month. It is more likely that it was news of the abdication, which took place on 21 November, and which also fits the timescale of Max's account. Max was writing only two or so years after the event in a memoir intended only for his family and had, therefore, little reason to distort the truth. Landau, on the other hand, was writing some sixteen years after the events he describes; he was also writing for publication, which may have influenced his recollections to make it appear that he was closer to the centre of affairs than was in reality the case.

Max's war was amost over. He spent the night in private accommodation in The Hague, and left for Rotterdam the following day. Malnourished, and, as he says, 'a babbling idiot' (and confirming, if only a little, Landau's impression of him), he stepped on to English soil once more at Gravesend on 26 November. But there still the matter of the proposal of the Hamburg Workers' and Sailors' Council.

Max was taken to London, where he met Cumming once more. Cumming was sufficiently impressed by the information that Max had brought out to arrange for him to see a group of senior officers in Intelligence – General Sir George MacDonogh (the Director of Military Intelligence), Ronald Campbell and Sir William Tyrell (both of whom were senior civil servants within the Foreign Office). Max wrote up the information in a report, but the Government never took up the plan which he had brought out of Germany. Landau recalled that Max had become more and more agitated during his debriefing, so much so that Landau began to suspect that his confinement had affected his mind. This may have influenced Landau's own report on the plan, and thus contributed to the Government's failure to act. More importantly, the idea of depriving Germany of all her important ports would have crippled any attempts to rebuild the country's shattered economy, and it was in the Allies' interests that Germany should be able to recover in order to be able to pay off the war indemnities which were to be imposed. Nor would the Government be keen to be working with the Bolsheviks on the Workers' and Soldiers' Council.

Max spent some time in a nursing home on his return before making the journey to Hull. On his arrival at his house in Coltman Street he spoke to each of his children in turn – his family could hardly recognise him, he was so emaciated. His daughter Gladys recalled, 'I remember Mother saying to us all, "I want you all to go out, and don't come back until about half past eight. And then you come back one at a time. And your father will be here." And so we all went out, and came back . . . And when I came in and went into the room and saw my father, who sat in one of the big green easy chairs. And what a shock I got. Instead of that wonderful, boisterous, hale, hearty – always had a good colour in his cheeks, and always well groomed, immaculate – and instead of that, here sat in this chair was a little wizened old man . . . It was a dreadful time.'

Although Max soon regained his former physical appearance, it may well be that he never really recovered from his ordeal. He had spent just over seven debilitating years in a foreign jail, to come home to find that he was no longer wanted by his former chiefs in intelligence, since his cover in Germany had been blown. Worse, he was to discover that, through no fault of his, not even his name was his own. He was no longer Max Schultz, but Max Hilton. The hostile attitude towards those of German ancestry demonstrated by the ugly scenes in Hull and elsewhere would take some years to heal – even the German Lutheran church in Hull remained closed until the 1930s (and then was forced to close again in 1939). Max's father died in 1921, his sister Clara and her husband continued to live in Germany, whilst his brother Charles had moved to Canada. Max tried to take up his yachtbroking business again, but the mood of the times was not in favour of the resumption of such extravagances.

Yet even now, with the war over, and Max no longer an Intelligence agent, his life was by no means empty of excitement. There was still time for family celebration. A correpondent of the *Daily Graphic* caught up with Max, at his daughter's wedding:

'The cheeriest man I met yesterday was a friend of mine who had been to a Northern port to attend a wedding. The bride's father was a well-known skipper who, while a prisoner in Germany for spying – he got two years' hard labour just before the war and was held over as an interned prisoner – conducted the naval revolution in Hamburg which really finished the war.

'My friend tells me that, more difficult though it is to conduct your daughter's wedding than a revolution abroad, the skipper's

The wedding of Max's daughter Beatrice. Max is standing fourth from the right, next to the bride. On Max's left is his daughter Gladys, and at the end of the line his daughter Clara. Sarah is seated second from the right, while George is seated on the ground at the right. Sarah's father George Hilton is standing second from the left.

essential English qualities even allowed him to compete the double event.'

But Max's life was still not without its dangers. One of Max's grandsons recalled, 'My father [George, Max's son] was once staying with his father in the Charing Cross Hotel in London. One night, Max told George to go into the bedroom and read a book; he shouldn't come out on any account, no matter what he heard. In the bedroom, George heard a bang, followed by the crash of broken glass. Looking out of the bedroom window, George saw that a man had fallen out of the hotel and fallen through the glass canopy over the door on to the

Max's grave in a Hull cemetery. He is buried with Sarah, and Sarah's mother and brother.

street below. But when he looked in the newspapers on the following day, there was no mention of the incident.'

It is impossible to tell what really happened here. Perhaps it was unfinished business from the war, or even from before. An account of British naval intelligence of this period, written by one of Cumming's former agents, Hector Bywater (Cumming referred to him by the codename 'H₂O'!) the author comments, 'The work itself was thankless, perilous and distinctly unremunerative, and those engaged in it too often found themselves caught in a web of intrigue and misunderstanding which has outlasted the war, and from which some may never hope to escape.'

Max knew this only too well. He died on 7 September 1924, just 49 years old.

Why were people like Max prepared to risk their lives in this way? In 1924, someone masking his identity behind the phrase, 'A Former Member of the Service', wrote a series of articles in the *Daily Telegraph*. Discussing his former comrades, he stated:

'It is safe to say that none of the survivors would ever dream of taking up Intelligence work again, under any consideration at all. The romantic associations of Secret Service exist largely in the imagination of writers who have had no experience of the real thing ... Every British member of the Intelligence Service abroad with whom I was acquainted took up the work, not in the hope of pecuniary reward, but from motives of patriotism, and in most cases only after urgent and repeated appeals by the I[ntelligence] D[epartment] chiefs in London.'

Even though we can only guess how Max was recruited, and his motives in agreeing to act as a spy, he may well have concurred with some of the sentiments expressed here. In his own words, 'I was a spy in Germany, and I am not only not ashamed of the fact, but proud of the risks I ran in getting information which I may fairly claim has helped us win the war.'

EPILOGUE: A MODEL AGAIN

When Peter Blühm found the note under the funnel of the *Imperator*, he went to the local newspaper, the *Hamburger Abendblatt*, both for help with the translation (as he did not speak English), and to see if they could shed any light on the shade of this English spy which had appeared in Hamburg. The *Abendblatt* got in touch with the local paper in Hull, the *Hull Daily Mail*. Max's relatives on both sides of the North Sea were shocked to see the model, about which they had known nothing, suddenly make the pages of their local papers.

It was not only Max's family who took an interest in the model. Prisoner-of-war models are very collectable objects in themselves, and the interest of a number of collectors was piqued by the news item. It is much to the credit of Herr Knölke that he insisted on giving first refusal on the restored model to Max's family, when he could have sold the ship to a collector for so much more (an offer of £5,000 was reportedly made). The families of each of Max's ten grandchildren contributed towards the purchase price, and were helped by a generous donation of £1,500 from Hull Museums. After 150 hours of careful restoration by Herr Blühm, the model now stands proudly in Hull's Maritime Museum.

Max's model, now restored by Peter Blühm.

The model is presented to Hull's Maritime Museum, with many of Max's descendants present, and, in the centre, Peter Blühm.

SOURCES

MANUSCRIPTS

Family Papers
Documents and photographs in the possession of Max's descendants

Public Record Office, Kew
FO 371/1126   Reports of the British Consul at Leipzig, 1911
RG11   1881 Census of Hull, enumerators' books
RG12   1891 Census of Hull, enumerators' books

Staatsarchiv, Hamburg
C27/27   Prison record of Prisoner 293 Max William Emil Schultz

NEWSPAPERS AND JOURNALS

Daily Graphic
Eastern Morning News
Hamburger Abendblatt
Hull Daily Mail
Isle of Wight Herald
The Pioneer
The Times

BOOKS

Andrew, Christopher. *Secret Service: the Making of the British intelligence community* (London, Heinemann, 1985).

Bywater, Hector & Ferraby, H. C. *Strange Intelligence: Memoirs of Naval Secret Service* (London, Constable, 1931).

Comfort, Richard A. *Revolutionary Hamburg* (Stanford, Stanford University Press, 1966).

Erkenhans, Michael. *Die wilhelminische Flottenrüstung* (Munich, Oldenbourg, 1991).

Gillett, E. & MacMahon, K. A. *A History of Hull* 2nd edition (Hull, University of Hull, 1989).

Heckstall-Smith, Anthony. *Sacred Cowes or, the Cream of Yachting Society* (London, Wingate, 1955).

Herzig, A. *et al. Arbeiter in Hamburg* (Hamburg, Erziehung von Wissenschaft, 1983).

Judd, Alan. *The Search for C: Mansfield Cumming and the Founding of the Secret Service* (London, Harper Collins, 1999).

Kelly's Directory of Hull various dates 1885-1921.

Landau, Henry. *All's Fair: the Story of the British Secret Service behind the German Lines* (New York, Putnam, 1934).

Lloyd's Register of Yachts (London, Lloyd's of London, annually).

Marder, Arthur K. *From the* Dreadnought *to Scapa Flow* (Oxford, Oxford University Press, 1961).

Massie, Robert K. *Dreadnought: Britain, Germany and the Coming of the Great War* (London, Cape, 1992).

Occleshaw, Michael. *Armour against Fate: British Military Intelligence in the First World War* (London, Columbus, 1989).

Rimell, Raymond L. *Zeppelin!* (London, Conway, 1984).

Schröder, Carl. *Aus Hamburgs Blütezeit* (Hamburg, Agentur des Rauhen, 1922).

Victoria County History of the East Riding Volume 1: the City and County of Kingston-upon-Hull (London, Institute of Historical Research, 1969).

Woodhouse, D. G. *Anti-German Sentiment in Kingston-upon-Hull: the German Community and the First World War* (Hull, City Records Office, 1990).